total
flirt

Also by Violet Blue

Seal It with a Kiss
Tips, Tricks and Techniques for
Delivering the Knockout Kiss

total
flirt

tips, tricks &

techniques every

girl needs to

get the guy

Violet Blue

VIVA
EDITIONS

Published in the United States by Viva Editions,
an imprint of Cleis Press Inc.,
2246 Sixth Street, Berkeley, California 94710.

Printed in the United States.
Cover design: Scott Idleman/Blink
Cover photograph: Digital Vision
Text design: Frank Wiedemann
First Edition.
10 9 8 7 6 5 4 3 2 1

Library of Congress Cataloging-in-Publication Data

Blue, Violet.
 Total flirt : tips, tricks, and techniques every girl needs to get the guy / Violet Blue. -- 1st ed.
    p. cm.
 ISBN 978-1-57344-646-4 (pbk.)
1. Sex instruction for women. 2. Flirting. 3. Seduction. I. Title.
HQ46.B577 2011
306.73--dc22
                                    2010049410

For BLM

CONTENTS

BE A DIVA

To me, flirting skills always seemed like one of those mysterious assets that a girl was either born with or not. Some girls just had it, like a genetic trait. Or they didn't, and had to rely on other more tangible tools—or tricks—to enjoy the wonderful cat-and-mouse game known as flirting. For instance, if you were lucky enough to be conventionally attractive, or famous, or you had an obvious physical feature that gave you an advantage, flirting skills were simply not needed.

As time went by and I shyly got to know my way around the dance of attraction that people do at parties, in bars and in one-on-one situations, I realized that my calculations had been a bit off. Sure, certain physical attributes could make a person seem superficially more interesting at first, but to flirt for more than a few short minutes, it takes more than being naturally blessed with a gimmick. Flirting, I would learn, wasn't something you are "just born with." Flirting is a skill you can learn. It's a craft, just like any other, and I quickly realized that any girl can be a good, fun, brazen, sassy flirt.

Half of flirting is the desire to flirt with someone we find attractive, and the other half is knowing how to use the tools of the flirting trade. Our desire to connect with someone cute or foxy gives us motivation, and our body, mind, and conversational skills make a flirty encounter a fun, adventurous reality.

Flirting isn't just for making that initial connection; flirting wears many hats. It makes us feel sexy and attractive, or gives us a feeling of satisfaction and self-reliance. It can ease the pain of heartbreak or bolster our ego when we're down. Flirting can pave the way for us to meet new people, find friendship, have one-night stands, help us find "the one," or just make an evening a lot more interesting. It can be about sex, or not about sex at all. Sometimes flirting is used as a tool to get free drinks, make others envious, or find out information about someone or something. For some people, it's just a way of socially communicating, and nothing more. It can be a great way to bond with girlfriends and guyfriends. For everyone, it's just good, clean fun.

No matter what your motivating factors are, this book gives you the tools to become a flirting diva. Or, if you're not the diva type, you'll find it laced with humorous personality tests and wild caricatures of flirty personas that you can use for inspiration or just for laughs. You'll learn how to walk like a siren, talk like a bombshell, seduce like a vamp, and even how to do all this on the Internet.

Here you'll find ridiculously funny one-liners and practical conversation starters for every purpose, no matter where you are or what you're doing—even if you're buying embarrassing personal products at the drugstore. Fine-tune your voice to its sexiest timbre, see how using your hands can hypnotize onlookers, and master the skill of speed flirting—it's all here. Feel shy, or not so confident? Kind of dorky or too big? No problem—there are oodles of confidence cures for a variety of situations, feelings, and doubts. And if you've ever had a flirting disaster, whether flirting with someone's boyfriend, saying something you really shouldn't have, or stepping on the hostess's prized poodle, you'll appreciate the entire chapter devoted to flirting disasters. You'll also find that no matter how you identify yourself, from shy and sweet personas all the way to devastating man-eaters and supervillain-esses, there are flirting techniques for all.

This is a guide for everyone who wants to flirt and have some sexy fun—and while the tone of the book is primarily geared toward women, I want to make it clear that everyone is warmly welcome here, and you will find this sentiment reflected in the text. I know that the cues and techniques of lesbian and gay male flirting (and cruising) are different from those of the female–male attraction game, enough so to fill a volume on each. I'm not going to make a pithy blanket statement that the techniques here are the same for all orientations. That's ridiculous. But I will say that if there's a bit of dishy diva in you, then you'll get a kick from the flavor of the text. And the body language clues, ideas for introductions, and humorous take on dealing with flirt disasters can certainly give anyone a good starting point for their adventures.

Use this book to enjoy life to the fullest, and to flirt like a delightfully wicked fiend. Celebrate your boldest dreams and fast-forward to the fun times, whatever your style.

Violet Blue
San Francisco

1 | FEMME FATALE FLIRT

Flirting can be deliciously sweet, like a juicy peach on a hot summer day. Flirting is wicked. Flirting is naughty. Most of all, flirting is fun. Congratulations on your decision to join the legions of fun-loving flirts who can realign the earth's orbit with the perfect opener—or present a sweet, quiet smile that can stop any international man of mystery in his tracks. The world of mortal men can always use a few more supervixens to make the party more interesting. Start now, and soon you'll have an arsenal of tricks, treats, and slinky moves to reign as queen supreme of the dating scene, or to be that glittery girl who shines at the party. Or to find that blissful connection with someone you really like.

Whatever your experiences with flirting were in the past, the tips in this guide will provide oodles of fool-proof techniques for finding, enjoying, and keeping the attention of your man *du jour*. Your goals don't need to be world domination or creating an army of male slaves—though all skill levels and go-getters are encouraged to apply. Perhaps you're tired of being the too-quiet one in the group and for a change you'd like to be the man-magnet for an evening. Or maybe you're on the prowl for a down-and-dirty fling. No matter your motives, flirting is where you shine and celebrate yourself, your friends, and the life you have here and now, and make the most of how you connect with someone you find attractive.

Anthropologists have found that flirting follows universal patterns. From London nightclubs to the Amazon jungle, people use the same body language when they flirt. It's universal, and this indispensable guide shows you how. You don't even have to dress saucy to be a first-rate flirt; your powers to attract and seduce are your own secret weapon, one that you can use to strike at any time, in any place, in any guise. This book gives you practical tools to nurture your flirting powers, useful for a lifetime of being a femme fatale flirt.

The Flirting Game: Two Ways to Play

Flirting is a game that no girl should ever wait to play: you can play now or later, but flirting is too much fun to let the party pass you by. And besides, the legions of flirt fatales who enjoy the fruits of guys on tap could always use another talented secret agent to join in the quest for world domination (or the snaring of the sweetest heart in the sexiest package to keep all to herself).

The first step in our master plan is understanding the concept of flirting. Guys see girls who flirt in a number of ways: cute, sweet, annoying, sexually available (most guys mistake female attention for sexual interest), scary but exciting, thrilling, and slutty, or they're relieved not to be guessing whether you're interested at all. In later chapters you'll find out how to navigate all of these situations and turn them to your advantage, even if that turns into "get me outta here!"

The most important thing to know about the concept of flirting is that there are two ways to flirt. There is flirting for fun, and there is flirting with intent. Flirting for fun is when you use all those wickedly wonderful smiles, teases, eyelash bats—many but not all of the flirting skills detailed in this book—for a playful tête-à-tête with someone you think is cute but who is off the menu. They may be off the menu for a variety of reasons: because he has a girlfriend (naughty you!), or she's a friend of a friend, or he's your gay pal who flirts back with feeling and fun. You don't mean anything when you flirt for fun, except to feel saucy and make your friend feel the same. It's reserved for people who feel safe to flirt with.

Flirting with intent is when you flirt with a goal. Your "flirtee" is your prey, and you are the huntress. Flirting with intent is a lot of fun; it's when the person you flirt with could be more than a friend, and you want to find out what that "more" looks like. You are sure it looks sexy, and will look good on your arm. Flirting with intent is how we scope for dates and mates, and while it's not uncommon to go from "fun" to "intent" in the span of a few beverages, usually when we're going out to flirt with intent a conquest of some kind is already on our to-do list. It's when you flirt and you *mean it*.

Flirt fatales in the know already know this: flirting for fun and flirting with intent don't look or sound very different to your flirt target. Even when flirting with intent, our manner is playful and teasing. We may in fact be engaged in a serious attempt to assess someone's suitability as a potential date—and to advertise our own perfectness for this position—but we do not conduct this mate-selection process like a job interview. We exchange glances, smiles, jokes, compliments, and touches, not résumés and experience. (No, never experience, ahem.)

Use the valuable tips in this guide to help you culti-vate the perfect Flirt Mode for your goals. This guide is designed to help you meet your goals and avoid confusion. The initial stages of flirting with intent can look a lot like flirting for fun—and this similarity can be a source of confusion and misunderstanding.

Researchers have found that two-thirds of all flirting is initiated by women. Did you know? Get down with your bad self! Girl flirting is done so subtly and unobtrusively that most people think men take the initiative with sexual cues. Women use subtle cues and signals so discreetly that men are not consciously aware of them and so *men usually believe they have made the first move*. Many studies show that men are not consciously aware of female flirt signals to which they are clearly responding. You can call the shots anytime you feel like stepping into the game. So even if you come across a "pickup artist" who thinks he's "always closing the deal" when he's chatting you up— this guide will keep you on top of the flirting food chain, right where you belong.

Flirt Style Quiz: What Are *You* Wearing?

Before you even think of stepping out or online to flirt and slay hearts and minds, take a look in the mirror and adjust that—attitude. Sometimes even the most expert flirts need a little help putting on that drop-'em-dead flirt attitude. When you're getting ready, prep with your favorite rallying music, makeup, and hair (even if you're on the computer), a light pre-launch drink or snack, a few outfit changes, a bit of Zoolander in the mirror, and putting on your flirt style.

Wait—what style?! You've got a style and may not even know it. Each woman has what it takes to make 'em drool. What's your style?

You're flirting with a hottie—but suddenly you've got competition from another girl who tries to edge you out of the game. Which chick flick do you take your next move from?

A. *Carmen Electra's Aerobic Striptease DVD*
B. *Amélie*
C. *Mean Girls* or *Bring It On*
D. *Heathers*

When starting a conversation, you:

A. Wait to see who begins first, then add something when it's your turn.
B. Order drinks.
C. Pretend to cry and tell the detective you need to find out who killed your husband.
D. Cross and uncross your legs in a mini-dress while going "commando."

When you notice an attractive prospect, you usually:

> A. See if he catches your eye, bite your lip, and look away.
>
> B. Gulp your drink and belch out the word "hottie!"
>
> C. Size him up like a side of beef at the market.
>
> D. Hunt him like a wild animal.

You'd never lift your skirt:

> A. On the first date.
>
> B. Unless you get a lot of shiny beaded necklaces in exchange.
>
> C. Before 10 p.m.
>
> D. What skirt?

Your philosophy about flirting is:

    A. Mix and mingle, but don't overdo it.

    B. Drink, flirt, repeat, until dancing with potted plants.

    C. There's one born every minute, so they'll need to take a number.

    D. Every man has his place in the food chain.

You get ready to go out for an evening of flirting by:

    A. Applying subtle lip gloss.

    B. Going through five wardrobe changes while singing and dancing to an entire Lady Gaga playlist (even the remixes).

    C. Removing wedding ring, fixing lipstick, and practicing your "come hither" look in the mirror.

    D. Surveying bedpost notches and emitting a fearful cackle while overcome with evil satisfaction.

When going out to flirt, you always make sure you have:

- A. Your cell phone for gathering contact info.
- B. A chaser.
- C. Condom, compact, a wig, and an alibi.
- D. One-way directions to your dungeon, printed neatly on business cards.

Your scariest nightmare about flirting includes:

- A. Being rejected in front of a group of people.
- B. Big streaks and handprints from your self-tanner on your back and neck.
- C. A man who can play you like a violin.
- D. Rainbows, unicorns, butterflies, puppies, and pantsuits.

IF YOU ANSWERED MOSTLY "A,"
YOU ARE A SWEETHEART.

You know that a coy smile can be more penetrating than an X-Ray, more powerful than She Hulk, and sexier than underwear ads. Subtle and sly, your style is less wallflower and more quiet seductress waiting to make her move. You don't need flashy tricks or silly one-liners; your power is in your eyes, voice, and hips—just like Wonder Woman in her everyday guise. A few refining touches and the librarian lets down her hair—and brings down the house.

YOUR FLIRT MANTRA IS:
"LET ME SHINE FOR YOU."

IF YOU ANSWERED MOSTLY "B," YOU ARE A DIVA.

Life of the party? Sure, if it means grinding on the dance floor in a shirtless hunk sandwich. It's all fun and games for you, lusty lady, and the center of attention is where you glow the hottest. You like to surround yourself with great conversation, smart fashion, a little gossip, and a hint of drama—which sometimes means you have to stand in front of a four-way mirror. With the right nurturing, your flirting skills will draw enough bees to your honey to make you feel like the queen you are.

YOUR FLIRT MANTRA IS:
"GIMME SOME SUGAR, BABY."

IF YOU ANSWERED MOSTLY "C," YOU ARE A FEMME FATALE.

You are temptation in a red dress, and your magnetic powers have brought down many a good man, and a few not-so-good men, too. Your wit is fiery, your neckline a plunging five-alarm fire, and every step you take spells "man-trap." If he can outwit you, he can have you—until you get bored. Hone your flirting skills, and get ready to put 'em in their place.

YOUR FLIRT MANTRA IS:
"TAKE NO PRISONERS—UNLESS THEY'RE CUTE.
THEN I'M THE WARDEN."

IF YOU ANSWERED MOSTLY "D,"
YOU ASPIRE TO BE A RULER OF ALL MANKIND.

You were the one in the leather catsuit who drove Batman to the brink of horny madness—and Robin is next. Men are your playthings, and they love every minute of it. Soon you will have created an army of male sexbots, and world domination will be yours. Sharpen your claws on this book, and woe to the next clueless stud you have for breakfast.

YOUR FLIRT MANTRA IS:
"I MAY BE BAD. BUT I *FEEL* GOOD."

Now that you're getting clear on your personal flirting path, it's time to learn the right moves, lines, and expert tricks to dial up your flavor of the moment. You may "click" with one of the four flirt styles above, or you may be the kind of girl who likes to mix and match her style. In the next few chapters we break down the basics so you can pick and choose the flirt style to go with every outfit, every occasion, and every guy who piques your interest. And even when your VIP flirting skills get you to the front of the line, they can also be your secret backdoor exit passes that get you out of sticky situations that might arise when you showcase your irresistible skills. You're about to get that all-access pass to any party you want in to, and all the tricks you need to accessorize it for full effect. Remember: it's always better to be flirty than forgotten. Turn the page for moves he'll never forget.

GET NOTICED, BE WANTED

C'mon, the party's dull—why not take a stroll across the room to get some ice and give the boys whiplash? Flirting begins the second you enter the room, or when you get up to seduce the snack table. When you make your entrance, whether subtle, dramatic, or even slipping on a loose floor rug, you're speaking volumes without even opening your mouth. First impressions, entrances, and opening conversations are all potential opportunities that can't be wasted. Within minutes, your prospects will have sussed you out and decided whether *you're* a prospect as well. Remember that you are here for a purpose, and your goals—whether economic (free drinks), mental (the cute one is *mine*), emotional (worship me), or physical (worship me all over)—will keep you on track for success. Get noticed by all the guys and narrow down the playing field as you go along.

Body language is truly the language spoken by all, and you send messages to everyone who looks at you, whether you mean to or not. Make sure your body language gives him the right idea. It's true what they say: you project an image depending on how you feel. The way you feel inside is unconsciously messaged to people around us by the way we hold our heads, hunch our shoulders, place our arms, present our facial expressions, sit, and walk. And every person alive, to some degree, can read and pick up on what our bodies are saying about our internal state of mind. It's instinctive.

There's nothing worse than desperately wanting to meet and flirt with someone, and having him pick up a desperation vibe from you. What not many people know is that it's easy to project any "vibe" you want.

When you learn a few essential tricks, sending direct and intentional body language messages is as easy as changing channels on a TV.

Get into Flirt Mode

Make the most of the effective flirting supertool known as body language. First, examine what you're projecting without even trying—then play around with saying exactly what you want without even opening your mouth. Look at how your body moves naturally and try out a few subtle changes that, in mere seconds, will take you from being passed over to fending off passes all evening long.

Stand or sit in a chair before a mirror and close your eyes. Take a few deep breaths to relax, and then slowly open your eyes without adjusting your body. Look at the position of your head, shoulders, arms, and legs. Another great way to look at your unconscious body language is to look at pictures taken of you when you were unaware of the camera. What is your body saying? Are your shoulders rounded, tummy forward, head down?

It's time to learn trick number one for your checklist: how to turn on your Flirt Mode. Each of these small adjustments can be made slowly, in a room full of people, and imperceptibly: even though you haven't said a thing, you will appear more confident. These are the techniques celebrities use whenever they are in public and want to go from no one to noticed—and you can make the most of them, too.

HERE'S HOW

Pull your shoulders back and take a deep breath, imagining your breath pulling your chest wider and pulling the center of your chest up toward the ceiling. Straighten your back and arch the lower back slightly—a good way to do this (and make your legs appear longer and your butt more attractive) is to wear heels. Even small heels will give you the advantage. Pull your head up and back slightly. Just these tiny adjustments will change everything.

When you make your flirt-mode stance, you're

going to project an aura of confident, relaxed, and happy. Maybe secretly you feel like a dork, nervous, silly, mad, worried, or cranky. No one needs to know your inner feelings when you shift your body just as I described; these subtle techniques project an air of strong self-knowledge and an aura of magnetism. Body language is *that* powerful. Try to remind yourself regularly throughout the day or evening to straighten, tilt back, and open your chest.

MORE MODE: SLOW DOWN

Add to your stance a slight, general slowing down of your gestures; cross and uncross legs in no hurry, lift your glass to your lips slowly, and don't rush to do anything. Quickness and hurried gestures make us appear less confident, and looking more self-assured will get you attention, fast. He'll want to know, who *is* that girl?

MAKE AN ENTRANCE IN MODE

When you walk into a room, get out of a car, get up to visit the loo, or enter a crowd, you're making an entrance—so do it in Flirt Mode. You're the person everyone wants to get to know, and you haven't even said a word. Let your friends enter first; the best is saved for last, and that's you. Take a moment to savor your entrance: stop before you start. This means you begin to get up or enter, then pause for a second to look around as if you might see someone you know. (It doesn't matter whether you actually see anyone you know—if you do, pause again to smile slowly and brightly.) If you have to keep moving when you come in, make your glance around the room last for two to three long strides.

If you're really feeling up for fun, make eye contact with a few of the people near you and smile at them. It doesn't matter whether they smile back. Or you can smile at one of your friends. The important thing is to enter the room grabbing attention, and smile like it's your party. From here, the boldest, most atten-tion-grabbing move is to walk to the middle of the room before settling on a spot to stand. Or you can walk forward, doing your room survey, and head to a spot that looks like a terrific vantage point for people-watching while remaining in the center of activity. Never retreat to the edges unless you want to be left alone to regroup, make a to-do list of names, or simply bask in your overwhelming desire to make men your lapdogs.

FLIRT MODE CHECKLIST

When the time is right, go into Flirt Mode.

❏ Get into the mode: head up, shoulders back.

❏ Move in mode: slow down.

❏ Wait one beat: stop before you start.

Prescriptions for Flirting Success: Confidence Cures for Every Girl

———

To get your career as a femme fatale flirt launched in style, you'll need to master the use of one secret weapon that works anywhere, anytime, and in any outfit, from stilettos to sneakers—confidence. Easier said than done, you say? Like a trademark logo, confidence lets your flirt targets know immediately that there is something special about you, and acts like a homing beacon for interested parties. Confidence need not be brash or flashy. It can be subtle, sophisticated, or powerful—and it doesn't matter what you look like, how you really feel inside, or how klutzy you are. It is the key element of your most effective flirting techniques.

Confidence, no matter who's got it, is always an act. It is a learned behavior, faked until it's second nature. Ask any actress and she'll tell you how scared she was the first time she got onstage, but she just acted confident, fooling everyone. Focus, darling. A focus on behaving confidently helps you keep sight of your goals while you act like the queen of the universe (even if you feel like hiding or running in tight little circles screaming), and it keeps you motivated. Pay no attention to the critics inside your head. Proceed with confidence through any room, any conversation, and you'll be projecting enough internal strength to make your critics disappear.

But what if you don't feel confident? Don't you wish there were some pill you could take? Well, there almost is. Read on, because the doctor is in.

YOUR SYMPTOM: You feel shy.
YOUR CONFIDENCE CURE:

- Look at your favorite pictures of yourself.

- Get together with your closest girlfriends and have an indulgence party: eat ice cream from the carton, tell each other how great you are, and watch episodes of *Glee*.

- Get a spa treatment.

▸ Practice the Flirt Mode body language techniques—fake it until you make it.

▸ Think about what you have to lose by holding back—opportunities galore.

▸ Before going out, get your girl power on by imagining you have an audition for *Idol* or *ANTM*. Crank up your favorite tunes, get in front of a mirror, and lip-synch and dance like Beyoncé in her Destiny's Child era. Mojitos optional.

▸ Create a new identity for yourself when flirting—take it as far as you want. Make up a fun and flirty name (Ruby Delicious, Brandy Alexander, Saucy Cupcake), affect an accent, wear a wig, and wear someone else's clothes. Try more name generators in chapter 6.

YOUR MOVIE TREATMENT: Ginnifer Goodwin in *Mona Lisa Smile*.

YOUR SYMPTOM: You feel like a dork.

YOUR CONFIDENCE CURE:

▸ Use your dorkiness to its fullest advantage. Practice "accidents" that involve spilling your drink in front of attractive partygoers, having to lean over and pick up the contents of your purse in a low-cut blouse, and always wear frilly panties that are "accidentally" seen in case you trip over floor rugs.

▸ Pretend you are a doctor and perform "examinations" on anyone hot.

▸ Dorks are sexy, brainy beauties who don't follow the pack. Wear lipstick with your glasses, a G-string under your corduroy pants.

▸ When you do something especially dorky, smile big like Miss America and take a bow.

▸ Learn to strut like a hot mama so you can trip over your own big feet with savoir faire.

▸ Remember that out there, somewhere, there is a dork for you who also happens to look like an international male model. The rest are just for fun—so on with the show!

▸ Intentionally say the wrong thing to get the conversation going—it's all good from there. Start with: "Is that your real hair?" "I really like you. I think guys with crooked teeth are cute." or "Do I have cocktail weenie breath?"

YOUR MOVIE TREATMENT: Janeane Garofalo as Baby Bowler in *Mystery Men*.

YOUR SYMPTOMS: You feel scared / angry / sad instead of fun.

YOUR CONFIDENCE CURE:

▸ Wear something fabulous to mask your inner feelings.

▸ Make a voodoo doll of the person who is making you feel bad and keep it in your purse. Feel bad, poke with sharp pin, repeat, smile!

▸ Try not to think of what is making you feel unpleasant. Instead, imagine having the ultimate revenge in a rain of destruction as you advance toward your next victim, er, flirt target.

▸ Blame others for your agony, and drown your sorrows in a tall, cool drink of a handsome stranger.

▸ Find out how to fake body language that will project confidence, rather than reveal your simmering sea of inner turmoil. Pull yourself together in a flash with the tips in the next section.

▸ Make a set of business cards with your contact info to give to hotties, in case you need to leave quickly to have a good cry.

▸ If you're afraid or nervous, imagine the "cool" people at the party naked. Or naked and begging you for mercy while suspended over a pit of ravenous alligators.

YOUR MOVIE TREATMENT: Uma Thurman as Poison Ivy in *Batman Returns*.

YOUR SYMPTOM: You have no idea what to say to anyone.

YOUR CONFIDENCE CURE:

▸ Find someone attractive and ask him who he knows at the party / event / monster truck rally.

▸ Questions are the key to getting people to open up and engage with you. Ask someone what he or she thinks about anything, and you've started a conversation. Find more openers in chapter 4.

▸ See if you can help organize or run the event or party. It's easier to "work it" if you're actually working it.

▸ Pretend you are blind and ask to "feel" the faces of cute guys. Let your fingers do the walking.

▸ Pretend you are foreign and ask attractive targets for information, such as where the drinks are, where the kitchen is, and so on.

▶ Take a deep breath, relax, and *almost* spill your drink on someone you think is cute. Instant conversation!

YOUR MOVIE TREATMENT: Brittany Murphy in *Clueless*.

The Inner Sexy Makeover for Every Body

Many have been propelled to flirt magnificence through the tremendous power of inner sexy make-overs. A favorite of ruling queens of lost civilizations, unexpectedly sexy bookworms, sultry tough chicks, and girly vampire slayers, a sexy makeover gives you confidence and sexiness that emanates from you in waves. Whether your motivation is to be the brightest star in the room, make him eat from the palm of your hand, or choke a man with your bare thighs, you are only the shell of a femme fatale flirt until you sex it up from within.

Your body is your temple, and if you're going to get any worshippers you have to start the devotions yourself. Splurge on a massage to get in touch with your body and to enjoy the healing touch of a massage therapist—it does wonders for body confidence, as do dance and body movement classes.

Sure, you say. *But I'm a dork! My body isn't a temple, it looks like Stonehenge!* And you're speaking for almost everyone—except those who've given themselves an inner sexy makeover. The makeover starts when you think about what bothers you. Chances are high your concerns boil down to a few very normal anxieties:

I'M WORRIED THAT I'LL LOOK RIDICULOUS.

Plan your strategies, learn seductive body language, try on your outfits and makeup ahead of time, and you can't miss. If you have a plan, the only thing he'll see is someone sexy who feels confident and enjoys life. He'll also be interested to talk to you. The only thing that might show is nervousness, but that will disappear after the first few minutes.

WHAT IF I SCREW IT UP?

Make your strategies "idiot proof" by going over all of the tools in this book step-by-step, repeatedly, and don't leave anything to the last minute. Take every precaution to make sure that you feel comfortable and sexy in your outfit, have a few topics to chat about, and a backup plan for what to do if you don't instantly connect (especially at a public gathering). If you're klutzy, be prepared to distract him by laughing when you trip over the host's prized poodle, and smile wickedly at your prey when you spill your Mimosa all over the hors d'oeuvres, as if to say, "I meant to do that. Watch me now!" A sense of humor layered with a sense of erotic purpose and determination will make him forget all about the spilled drink—especially if you reveal a bit of cleavage when you mop it up with all the napkins meant for the guests. Plus, ripped stockings are quite sexy.

MY BODY ISN'T WHAT I WANT IT TO BE.

Join the biggest club in the world. Everyone feels this way on one level or another, even the "perfect" people. If you don't like it, make a plan to change it. If you can't change it, *work it*. You've got a sexy boy toy lined up as your erotic plaything: this situation won't be around forever, so make the most of what you've got to offer. Chances are high that you're a lot sexier than you think, because sexy comes from inside, not outside. Just ask any stripper who performs during her period—and they all do. If you're worried about "stacking up" to others, be it with breast size or other measurement concerns, remember that bigger boobs won't make you sexier, they'll just make you someone with big boobs. And yes, people can be insensitive and say inappropriate things. If you find yourself mistakenly flirting with one of these clueless critics, change the channel and flirt with someone worthy.

In the world of flirting, exotic dancers (strippers) are to the rest of us what the Amazons were to Wonder Woman: overkill to the world of mortals, but a powerful source of inspiration and clever tricks. While some might consider onstage gyrations and pole dancing to be too blatant, or even ho-hum, these women have mastered the art of walking into a room and making themselves the sexual center of attention (nudity notwithstanding). The point is, these gals were once like the rest of us, but now they can turn on a whole room with a smile and a flip of their hair—and chances are good they can do it with their clothes on, too.

So, you have to wonder, how did those girls get

from where you are to up there on that stage? And what can you learn from them?

First of all, they have learned to accept what they've got. Because we think people have narrow definitions of hotness, we forget that everyone has the same complaints about themselves. Actual sexy people don't look like packaged porn stars or Hollywood types *in real life*—come to think of it, most of those people look a bit odd in real life. The girls who work the poles have fired their inner critics, for at least a few songs anyway. Time and time again, it works, because confidence and sexiness in real life is riveting.

Even Marilyn Monroe could walk down the street without makeup and go unnoticed. One day while strolling with a reporter, she remarked that a femme fatale only needs to adjust her body language to be recognized by anyone. In two seconds she straightened up, walked her signature walk, smiled, and moved her body just so—and was soon surrounded by fans. Take your cues from Marilyn's ability to go from zero to 60 with a smile and wiggle. Then try it at home.

Show, Don't Tell

Your first step in becoming the most magnetic woman in the room is to assemble an image to project. Borrow bits and pieces of your look and moves from celebrities you admire, friends you consider confident or sexy, and women in history who have brought about the downfall of mankind. Consider hairstyle, makeup (or lack of), grooming details such as well-kept hands and feet, and style of dress.

▸ If someone has told you that you look like a celebrity you find attractive, examine the details of their personal appearance; or look at other gorgeous women who possess physical traits (facial features or body shapes) similar to yours. Copy what looks sexy: hairstyle, makeup, clothes, posture, or facial expressions.

▸ Do some personal care grooming on a semiregular basis. Get a mani- or pedicure (or give yourself one), have your eyebrows shaped (or buy a stencil kit), and enjoy a facial once in a while. Ramp up your daily look just slightly, so you won't have to find a phone booth to become Wonderflirt if you see an especially magnificent specimen at the Laundromat.

▸ Watch other skilled flirts and sexy vixens closely to see how they smile, make eye contact, hold their head, and laugh. These skills are a snap to make your own. Take notes, because you'll find more on these techniques in chapter 3.

▸ Make the most of your sexy friends, who will become your allies and minions. Ask them what makeup, hair products, and personal services they use, and find out where they shop.

▸ Dressing for sexy comfort is key, but never fret if you have to use your powers without your femme fatale outfits. When you do go out to conquer, wear something sexy *and* comfortable—never sacrifice one for the other.

▸ Makeup is not necessary, yet can be a powerful tool. Use with discretion. The most essential item in your arsenal is lip gloss, or supple-looking lips. Smooth, shiny, or rouged lips will magnetize at 50 yards. Exfoliate your lips with a toothbrush regularly, moisturize with lip balm, and find a shade of gloss that can go from day to night. Don't be caught without it, even if you aren't wearing anything else. Gloss, no matter what's in style, is like waving a red flag at hapless bulls.

Pussycat Walk: Flirt Mode in Motion

They say you have to walk before you can fly, and in flirting, you have to learn to walk like a siren from planet man-eater before you can start planning on where the notches in your bedpost are going to go. The Pussycat Walk is your Flirt Mode in motion, and every girl can do it. Like overall body language, your

walk speaks volumes to whoever is watch
the right body language can wake 'em up wł
someone sexy isn't paying enough attention. Yɛ
create confidence as fast and as easily as using the tips
for physical attitude adjustment in the section "Get
into Flirt Mode" earlier in this chapter. The icing on
your confidence cupcake is a sexy walk. With a few
subtle shifts in your gait, the Pussycat Walk can take
your already confident persona into the stratosphere.

Before you change anything, observe the way other
girls walk, especially ladies you think look sexy. Celebrities, friends, even 10 minutes in a park will give you
much to watch and learn from. Look at how well, or
badly, people walk. Take notes, and decide to try out
moves you like.

PUSSYCAT WALK

Flirt Mode and Pussycat Walk are your own secret weapons. You walk like a Pussycat when you:

▸ Walk the (imaginary) line: one foot directly in front of the other.

▸ Head up: don't look down unless you need to.

▸ Arms straight, shoulders in soft motion.

▸ Slow it down: you're too cool to rush.

As in the Flirt Mode lesson, begin by taking a look in a mirror at the way you walk; tweak it with a few small adjustments, and let the sparks fly. Find a full-length mirror, and walk toward it. Pay attention to your head, shoulders, hips, legs, and how your feet hit the floor. Do you sort of bob up and down when you walk? Swing your legs in a gait, or fast and anxious? Is your upper body "frozen" when you walk? Now stand still, look in the mirror, and add some Pussycat movement. Lift your head up, square your shoulders, and loosen your hips and arms. Stand in place, swinging your arms back and forth to free them up. Swivel your hips in a figure-eight motion, like a belly dancer. Now you feel silly. But you look marvelous. A panther, ready to pounce.

Now walk the line, Pussycat. Imagine an invisible line painted on the ground, and try to aim each step loosely on that straight line. Lead with your hips, rolling one side forward at a time with each leading leg. You don't need to exaggerate or pretend you're on a tightrope; try the subtle approach. Imagine the line stretching in front of you, or practice on an actual line on the ground. Try it with yarn, or a line of tiles on the floor. Sobriety tests don't count.

Keep your shoulders back, as in Flirt Mode; this is a physical way to say you are open to meeting new people. Open to new adventures = open your shoulders. Imagine a corset squeezing your waist oh-so-sexily, and straighten up your back. Follow each Pussycat step by bringing the opposite shoulder softly forward, creating an attractive, serpentine movement. Left leg, right shoulder; right leg, left shoulder. Leave your arms loose and relaxed, moving on their own as you walk. If you're carrying a purse, do so in whatever way that allows your arms to hang freely, with elbows unbent; and if you have an object to carry, try to hold it below hip level. Oh yeah, baby. You know why.

Keep your gaze level, your face relaxed, and move a second or two slower than usual. Stare straight ahead, not at the ground or up at the sky. To keep your head level and chin up, it really does help to practice walking with a book on your head. Draw yourself up, imagine being bigger and taller than anyone else in the room, and even if you're not, you'll appear to be. Shoes with heels draw attention to legs, hips, and butt—use this power with discretion. Now breathe, Pussycat.

SILENT SEDUCTION SECRETS: FLIRT WITHOUT WORDS

Now you're ready to bring your inner femme fatale flirt to the party. You have a can't-fail checklist to give you all the right moves, and a walk to hypnotize any man you want to make into your plaything. Now it's a matter of reeling him in. And with these techniques, you don't even need to say anything, just yet.

Some features, especially certain very sexy features we already possess, can make us the most magnetic girl for miles. Even if it's a bad hair day, you forgot to draw on your eyebrows, or you just sat on a wet barstool. After all, what is a flirt queen without an alluring smile, captivating eyes, sexy legs, and hands that say everything you wouldn't dare to—or maybe some very flirty things you *will* say when you decide to cast your spell.

 ## The Eyes Have It

Your eyes meet across the room. Girl, the game is on—you can relax, because you're just getting warmed up, but locking gazes (even if for a second at a time) is the foundation for every spell you're about to cast. Relationship and dating experts consider eye contact to be the most effective tool for flirting success. People instinctively know when someone is checking them out. And when instinct meets direct eye contact, your flirt target can actually experience a physical, erotic rush. Your eyes are your most remarkable weapons, able to unleash flirting abilities the world has never seen. Used properly, a careless glance can inflame the desires of every man, goldfish, and houseplant in the room—and possibly inanimate objects as well.

Eye contact will always be the center of your game. Every move you make hinges on what you do with your eyes. If you stare at the ground, no guy will think you are interested, or *interesting*. Anyone can look at another person—but someone special makes eye contact with them.

If making eye contact seems daunting, try a few exercises and learn a few cheaters that'll make you comfortable with looking directly at the man (or men) you're hot for. Pay attention to what you look at next time you walk through the office, a café, or the parking lot on the way to your car. Notice where your eyes naturally roam, whether you look at the ground, the sky, or if you skip your eyes around to look at objects. In particular, how are you looking at people—are you looking at their legs, feet, hands, or faces? Practice focusing your gaze directly level, at about the point people's faces would be. When you feel good about it, glance at an attractive man's face for a moment, and then back in front of you. You did it—now do it a few more times until you get the hang of it.

Your next lesson in eye contact for the shy is to

practice on a real-life sexy guy, in a conversation. You don't need to stare raptly into his eyes until your eyes dry out and your eyelids twitch and you start to see little fuzzy things out of the corners of your eyes. Instead, allow your eyes to travel around his face slowly, like a second hand sweeping around a clock from noon to midnight. Rest on his eyes, and begin again. Do this whenever you feel nervous about looking into his eyes for too long, and soon you'll be captivating him with your confident gaze before you even realize it.

But wait, there's more. Eye contact is a finely honed technique for mesmerizing hotties, and you're going to learn to wield it like Xena's sword, or Buffy's stake. Try an experiment in eye contact, and think of it as exercise—as though eye contact with intent were a muscle you're learning to make stronger. Pick a day when you're feeling sassy and make eye contact with sexy total strangers—at least two. Five in a day, then you're at the next level: making deliberate eye contact with men you find attractive. Try it once, and you'll see how easy and fun it is—no one gets hurt, rejected, and there's no risk involved. Try it again and again, like rehearsals, and you'll be ready to rock harder than Joan Jett.

Looks That Thrill

———

You don't have to be aggressive to reap the benefits from these eye contact flirt techniques—but being a bit brazen doesn't hurt. Think about the goal.

▸ When you have the beast in your sights, give your intended more than a glance. Let your eyes linger on his for a relaxed breath. Then decide if you want to keep contact for an intense across-the-room flirt, or move your eyes away to be a bit more playful in your approach.

▸ If he's playing hard to get, or you want to make him pay more attention, draw attention to your eyes by touching the corner of your eye as an adjustment, slightly touching the hair around your forehead, adjusting your glasses, or touching a pen to your temple.

▸ Make eye contact, and then break it to look at his lips, and then back again. Smile. This can be repeated with success throughout conversations.

▸ Truly bad girls will make eye contact, slide their eyes down the front of his body, and then back up. Extra brazen points for lingering on the chest or hips.

▸ Of course, maintaining eye contact when you need to blink is very sexy, and lets him know you don't want to miss a minute of his time.

Smile Sorcery

The easiest way to disarm, relax, and intrigue any man is with a smile. It sounds simple and corny, but when you're flirting, a smile dancing on your lips is an instant relaxer, and makes guys curious about what you're smiling about. A smile gives the unconscious impression that you have a great sense of humor, you're approachable, and being around you is safe and indicative of a good time. Yes, a smile says all that without words. Even a light smile while talking can make you appear that much more inviting.

Next time you people-watch, look around at how everyone is holding their mouths, and how it speaks volumes about your impression of them. Someone with tight unsmiling lips seems stressed, unfriendly. Another person might have a frown, or be posing with a serious mean look—no smile here, just unapproachable people. Find people in the crowd who are smiling, laughing, or have just the tiniest hint of a smile playing around the corners of their mouths. See how they look more attractive, friendly—like someone you might ask for directions if you were lost? We instinctively feel good around people who are smiling—and that's just how you'll want any potential flirt targets to feel when they look at you: at ease, relaxed, and warm toward you.

A smile does indeed weave a spell around you. But

you don't need to look like Faye Dunaway in *Mommie Dearest*, walking through the subway or standing at the snack table. No, a maniacal smile will send the opposite message, unless you are laughing and smiling like a loon for a reason. You just need the tiniest smile at the corners of your mouth to look sexy, happy, and open. Keep your lips closed, and gently curve the edges up in a half-smile: this is the sexy smile you'll use when you make an entrance, stroll sexily across a room, gaze at paintings, survey the last of the snack table's cheese in a can, or anything else you happen to be doing.

Our lips are one of the most suggestive, sensual erogenous zones we've got—and right on our faces. When a boy is interested in you, he'll look at your lips almost as much as your eyes. You can slyly direct him to look at your lips to subliminally suggest sex throughout your entire communication with him, no matter whether you're talking or not. Knowing that your lips look supple and shiny (see the section "Show, Don't Tell" in chapter 2), you can play around with what touches your lips, how they are touched, and what goes in and out of them. Bite your lower lip suggestively while smiling to tease and tempt. Rub them together softly and smile. Bite the end of your finger for a second—tilting your head down to do so is very flattering to your eyes and face. Touch your straw to them before you sip. Rub them lightly on the edge of a glass. If you're not sure he's paying attention, direct his gaze to your lips with a pen, a finger, a straw, a snack, a lollipop, or a fork.

Wear a soft smile like your lip gloss—remember to reapply every chance you get. But when you open your mouth to say anything, make sure you frame it with an even bigger smile. Smiling while you talk does a couple of neat tricks: it makes you easier to hear because it opens up your mouth to let more sound out (allowing you to speak in a sexy low tone without amplifying), and it makes anything you say seem instantly more fun. The talking smile lights up your entire face, gives you the appearance of seeming genuinely engaged with the man you're talking to, and makes him feel special—it's as if the act of talking to him is causing your happiness.

Then there is the ultimate smile to use as a devastating flirt tool, the smile of serious flirtation: the soft smile with eye contact that slowly transforms into a full smile with teeth exposed, all while staring and blushing like a fiend. This is the doomsday weapon you deploy when you want it bad, and you want him to know that you mean it. This smile can be wicked, naughty, and direct—or sweet, sublime, and joyously flirtatious. Either way, it sends a clear message: I want, I want, I want.

Never-Fail Techniques: Smile Styles

Use these devastating lip-loving techniques with discretion—many a man and civilization have been destroyed by such a smile.

TECHNIQUE #1, FOR SWEETHEARTS

Make eye contact, head slightly tilted, and smile halfway, then look away. Look back, keep eye contact, and smile your sweetly bad smile, big and with teeth exposed. Look away. Look back in a few seconds. Hook, line, and sinker, baby.

TECHNIQUE #2, FOR DIVAS

Make smoldering eye contact, head tipped slightly forward, using your soft smile. Maintain riveting eye contact and smile wide, keeping lips together. Now he is putty in your hands.

TECHNIQUE #3, FOR FEMME FATALES AND RULERS OF ALL MANKIND

Stare him squarely in the eyes, head level, with a soft smile playing across your lips. Smile the smile, unmoving, continuing eye contact and keeping lips together. Release the smile to let it down to half-mast. Arch an eyebrow invitingly. You have just employed a technique that has destroyed honest men, large coastal towns, and small nations—you have just transformed him from man to fearless minion, ready to do your bidding, or bedding.

THE FIVE ELEMENTS
OF WORDLESS SEDUCTION

▸ **EYES:** Use eye contact to spark interest.

▸ **MOUTH:** Give him a sweet smile so he sees how yummy you are.

▸ **HANDS:** Show him where to look, literally.

▸ **ARMS:** Open them to show that your mood is inviting.

▸ **FEET:** Set your tone with flirty playful movement, or pointed and eloquent.

The Surprising Power of Suggestion: Hypnotize Him with Your Hands

Our poor hands. We enslave them, make them wait on us, cook our food, clean up after us—and what do we give them? More work. And the whole time, they are saying, *We are sexy! Let us flirt!* Given the chance, your hands can be the flirting equivalent of Robin to your Batman, able to help in a pinch, pinch the help, and give your flirtee subtle signals that can seal the deal.

Your hands will silently, subconsciously tell him where he has to look—and you'll be surprised when his eyes obey. He won't even realize you're beaming suggestive signals about your sexiness directly into his brain. It's so simple, yet deliciously devious, and it totally works like a charm.

Use your hands to primp and adjust your look— here and there, not like *Girl, Interrupted*. Move your hands to direct where you want to focus his attention; nape of the neck, eyes, lips, cleavage, or lower. Straighten your collar, brush cat hair off your skirt or pants, smooth or move your hair back, coyly replace a fallen bra strap, or smooth out a wrinkled crotch.

Touch yourself in slightly suggestive ways, yet in ways that would never be *too* outrageous. Naughty girl—you can even pretend your hands are his eyes. In gay male cruising, the gestures are more overtly sexual, such as thrusting the hands into front pockets, with the thumbs pointed crotchward—though casual situations beg for more subtlety. If you are seated, rub your calves or smooth your hands over your legs. Take off a shoe and rub your ankle or foot, as feet are quite sexy. Rub your hands over your arms almost as if you are cold, but slowly. Glide your hand across the back of your neck, feeling the softness of your skin, and even give it a momentary gentle, stress-relieving rub. Rest your hands on your hips, or on your thighs. You don't have to touch yourself to send a super-sexy message, either. Caress a glass seductively, playing with the stem or circling the rim; stroke or knead a pillow.

Hand Commands He Can't Resist

———

Your hands can be very expressive. Not only can they play "follow the leader" with his gaze, they can also communicate your mood and set the tone for your overall body messages. Decode your hands' secret messages and tell 'em who's making the rules of attraction—you!

THE MESSAGE: DO ME!

▸ Relaxed hands, resting open and palms down on hips, suggest sensuality and comfort.

▸ Convey honesty and openness by positioning your arms so that your hands face palms out, exposing your inner wrists.

▸ It sounds simple, but wrists are sexy tools you can use to your advantage. We keep our wrists held inward toward our bodies in an unconscious protective manner, but turn your wrist outward to the hunk you're chatting up and you've subtly shared an intimate gesture.

▶ Sitting at a table with your arms stretched out toward your subject suggests a comfortable invading of space. Your arms out, palms up, suggests a bit of vulnerability and "reaching" toward him.

THE MESSAGE: MAKE HIM WORK FOR IT

▶ Conversely, clenched hands or hands gripping each other communicate stress, disinterest, or defensiveness.

▶ To give a hand signal of confidence and power, make a palm-down gesture when speaking, and form a "steeple" with all points of your fingers touching.

▶ A finger or two resting on the chin might communicate thoughtfulness and focus, but resting your chin in the palm of your hand says, "I'm bored now"—unless you're smiling; then your gesture says "sneaky."

▸ Holding your hand over your chest just above your cleavage suggests hiding your assets, yet it is a display of autoerotic touching. This says that you are a sensualist, but the touching is on your terms.

Your Arms:
They Communicate a Thousand Words

Your arms tell him how you're feeling; as I said in chapter 2, if they're bent or crossed, he won't get the message that you're open to his advances. Think of your arms as two long mood rings attached to your body—how you hold 'em and fold 'em tells the world whether you mean "clear skies" or you are a one-woman storm.

FULLY ARMED: Arms crossed across your chest (covering breasts) with fingers on backs of arms is the most protective, defensive posture possible.

    FORECAST: Can't touch this!

BOULDER HOLDERS: Arms are crossed beneath breasts or on lower rib cage, with hands on forearms. Pressing boobies together optional.

FORECAST: Cool and sexy.

HALF COCKED: One arm is crossed while the other hangs. Again, boob lift optional.

FORECAST: Heavy shyness, chance of flirting.

MONKEY GIRL: One arm is in motion, gently swinging as if to cross your chest and stay there, but you only fidget with your watch or shirt before returning it to your side.

FORECAST: Light shyness with scattered possibility of wild monkey sex throughout the night.

ON THE HUNT: Arms are relaxed and rest at sides, wrists exposed.

FORECAST: Casual flirt, using herself as the bait.

DEADLY WEAPONS: Hands are on hips with chest out and thumbs pointing toward crotch.

FORECAST: Man-eater. One-woman army.

Flirt Fail: Forgetting Your Feet

While you've been working to carefully create your arsenal of flirting techniques and super-secret ultra-magnetizing flirt rays, you may have had a pair of double agents working to undermine your best-laid plans to get...some action. These nefarious moles are actually your mules—your feet, that is. Your feet and legs tend to get left to their own devices when you're working the rest of your body into a flirt frenzy, and left alone, the consequences can foil everything. Curses, Catwoman! Use the following diagnostics to keep your footsies underfoot and your flirt strategies in total control.

SWEET SIDEKICKS: YOUR HELPFUL PARTNERS IN CRIME ARE WEARING THE MANOLOS.

- Standing or sitting, feet are pointed toward the hot guy.

- Legs cross and uncross, with feet toward him.

- One toe slips out of a shoe to cut class and play outside. A wonderfully dirty trick.

- Legs crossed, the naughty one on top swings slightly in and out toward your intended flirtee. You are the naughty one on top now.

- Standing, one foot is pointed at him, the other slightly to the side. Flirty, but you call the shots.

- Legs are stretched out, loosely crossed at the ankles: All is good: *I am confident and relaxed*.

▸ One foot does a little recon, sneaking forward to touch his toe for a moment as if an accident, then back. Good feet, doing the dirty work. Gauge his reaction.

▸ One foot sneaks up against his foot and applies a steady pressure. A time-tested trick used by expert foot flirts worldwide. See if he returns your pressure or moves away.

BAD DOGGIES: YOUR TOOTSIES ARE WORKING FOR THE ENEMY, OR GIVING AWAY YOUR PMS.

▸ Legs are crossed tightly.

▸ Legs are crossed so tightly you've cut off circulation to your ass.

▸ Legs wrap around each other several times like a pretzel or a painfully advanced Yoga posture.

▸ Knee bent to chest with arms holding it protectively. You are a ticking time bomb.

▸ Nervous fidgeting—toe tapping, shifting from foot to foot, rocking onto toes—says, "I'd rather be anywhere but here."

▸ Legs crossed with elevated foot swinging wildly. You drank too much coffee and have to pee, or are feeling defensive inside—and showing it.

Tips for the Flawless Wordless Approach

There are do's and don'ts to the silent star's flirty approach. They can be boiled down to *positioning* and *signaling*.

Positioning is the way you present yourself to Mr. Hot. Stand, don't sit (if you can avoid it). Stand in proximity to him; try not to be separated by more than two people. Face slightly away from him: this will make your signaling powerful. Stand like a Pussycat: no slouching, cock your hip. When you go out prowling with your girl crew, try to keep it just you and one or two friends so men don't get intimidated. And when you go to the bar, make your trips to order a drink solo.

Signaling is like waving the red flag to the bull, but much sweeter. It's the little things you do to get attention of the sexy kind. Toss your hair two or three times. Do the self-touching I explained in the hands section: your arms, collarbone, your hair. Look around a little: if you're facing slightly away from him, he'll be drawn to look at you (and feel safe doing so). Don't get too physically energetic or screechy-loud with your girlfriends, or he won't think you're open to approaching. Most of all, practice the eye contact and smile sorcery from this chapter, and try this formula: look down, smile at him, look down again, touch your hair, then look back at him. Then get ready to actually say something, hotness!

4 | KNOW YOUR LINES

Some people eschew opening lines when they share flirt advice or pickup techniques. But the truth is, when you open your mouth you're going to have to say something to make a connection. Your goal for effortless flirting is casual conversation with a romantic spark. It doesn't hurt that you also have dozens of nonverbal tricks up your sleeve (or in your purse). But when you're on the spot and the pressure is on, it's easy to freeze up and say something dorky, uttering a line that falls flat and leaves you standing there, wishing a natural disaster would occur immediately so you could at least be forced to talk about surviving through the next few minutes together.

Because life isn't always like the movies (okay, it almost never is), this chapter will make sure that no matter what, you always have something to say. So you'll have a few conversational tricks, a few cheesy opening lines, and a few backup topics handy when you feel like a deer caught in the headlights.

The Perfect Approach (Every Time)

You need to make what they call in science fiction movies "first contact." Mars, meet Venus; Harry, meet Sally; Sigourney, meet Aliens. Stand close to your flirt target (but not so close that he feels trapped) and make eye contact. Smile right away. If he avoids your eyes, or doesn't smile back, move on to the next prospect. But if he looks into your eyes, you're in; and if he smiles too, the game has begun.

He might start talking first, in which case you can follow his lead and off you go. You can tell that you should start talking if he doesn't say something within the first 3–4 seconds. Don't panic if you can't think of anything for a second; instead let your situation give you clues about what to say. You'll want your opening conversation to be ordinary, light, something that fits the situation you're in. Start with a question or comment on your surroundings or the world around you. Anything from "Is it cold in here, or is it just me?" to "Who are you with—do you know the hostess?" is fair game. Consider your situation and think of an opener before you make your approach.

The best thing to do in any situation with a stranger, especially one you want to flirt with, is to ask him about himself—then listen, and ask more questions. If your first opener doesn't go anywhere, move on to the next opener, and make it another question. People seldom meet others who are interested in their opinions, or want to know more about them, and it's a terrific way to get someone to like you instantly. Take it easy talking about yourself; if he asks you questions in return, it's a bonus. That means he's interested in you, too.

There are three main rules for starting a conversation with a sexy guy. First, stay away from negative comments because you never know what he might find upsetting—he might love those little dogs you're making fun of, or the creepy guy you're making jokes about might be his friend.

Rule number two: always follow a question with a question. Your job as the conversation starter is to keep it moving: if one opening question goes nowhere, follow it with one on a different topic. If, on the third try, your conversation still hangs in the air like a fart, make an excuse and move on to the next prospect (or to the bar, off to fix your look, and so on).

The final rule of starting conversation is to not invest too much in someone you just met. If he can't keep up the conversation, then you mistakenly picked a dud: move on. Either you "click" or you don't, and if the openers feel like weak one-liners, then you haven't found your match—keep looking.

The SIS Test

———

When you find yourself in a situation with someone you'd like to flirt with, before you turn on the flirt, size up the environment with the SIS test: sociability, icebreakers, and shared interests. This way, you'll know if the environment is ideal, and you can proceed with your techniques. The SIS test will also tell you if the situation you're in has challenges that you'll need to take into account, or if there are major factors working against you. A location with more SIS will make it easy to invent a reason to talk to your flirt target. Size up your location with the SIS test. The more your location passes the test, the better your chances of success.

SOCIABILITY: Is your location good for having a conversation with new people? Is it good for talking to strangers—for example, a bar, a party, a festival, or an online environment? Does the place have "public" space that's good for socializing, or is it made up of "private" zones, such as a bar with seating only at tables, making it difficult to meet and talk to new people?

ICEBREAKERS: Is there something to break the ice, like multiplayer video games, Rock Band®, a pool table, a photo booth, a dance floor, suggestive viewing (like music videos on TV monitors)? Icebreakers especially include social lubricants like alcohol, which lowers inhibitions and eases shyness.

SHARED INTERESTS: Is it a place for people who have a common interest or purpose? This could be a work-place (I know, taboo!), museum, school, conference, online community or social media website, dance club, sporting venue, hobby group, or volunteer event.

DEAD ZONES

According to research, supermarkets, the gym, public transit, parks, and theaters are places that almost always fail the SIS test. Don't get your hopes up in these single-unfriendly zones, hot pants!

Easy Opening Lines

——

Learn to deliver the lines that'll make him smile anywhere, anytime.

AT A PARTY:

- ▸ Did I need an invitation?
- ▸ Whose party is this?
- ▸ Are there any snacks?

AT THE BAR:

- ▸ Have you ever had a "screaming orgasm"?
- ▸ What is a customary tip in this country?
- ▸ When do the flamenco dancers arrive?

AT THE JUKEBOX:

- ▸ Any Poison or Willie Nelson in there?
- ▸ Is this in alphabetical order?
- ▸ If we shake it, does the money come out?

IN THE HEALTH FOOD STORE:

- ▸ If it goes in bright green, does it come out that way?
- ▸ Do vegetarians really taste better?
- ▸ Psyllium husks changed my world. For real.

IN A CAFÉ:

- ▸ Oops, I'm sorry—I thought that was *my* double half-caf caramel soy frappe!
- ▸ Can I borrow the humor section of the *Wall Street Journal* when you're through?
- ▸ Is it true that coffee is an aphrodisiac?

AT THE LAUNDROMAT:

▸ I hear soap is an aphrodisiac, too.

▸ Can I borrow six quarters?

▸ If my washer stops, will you be so kind as to put my panties in the dryer?

IN THE SUBWAY / AT A BUS STOP:

▸ I've been here for ten hours.

▸ I hear standing around is good for your circulation.

▸ I'm new to this city. Can you recommend a romantic place for dinner?

AT A FUNERAL:

▸ I'm so sad—hold me!

▸ Help me to feel alive again!

▸ I didn't know him very well, but now I appreciate life more than ever. Discuss?

IN A FOREIGN COUNTRY (TRANSLATE THESE EXCELLENT OPENERS):

- I am a virgin.
- Show me what love is.
- Under the table in this restaurant is fine.

AT A SWINGER'S CLUB:

- When do we put our clothes back on?
- Which one is your wife?
- I'm glad I brought a towel.

AT THE LIBRARY:

- Do you carry the works of the Marquis de Sade?
- You don't work here?
- Can we pretend that you work here?

AT A DINNER PARTY:

- I dropped my napkin under your chair.
- And my fork.
- My contact lenses too—mind if I feel around for them?

IN THE DRUGSTORE SHOPPING FOR TAMPONS, PREPARATION H:

- ▸ They really carry everything here!
- ▸ My grandma will be so glad I could do her shopping.
- ▸ My grandpa, too.

Is It Hot in Here, or Is It Me?
Opening Lines

———

It's like that dream where you're at the grocery store and you realize you're butt naked: you go through your flirt checklist, put on your Pussycat Walk, make contact, and then—you're speechless.

Never again. With all that hotness under your lid, you could probably blurt out any crazy-lady line and have him handing over his digits in seconds. But having actual opening lines will save your (not nekkid) butt every time.

If you're feeling crafty, there are two types of chat-up lines for getting you started: these lines will help you meet him *and* learn more about him by starting a conversation so you can size him up—things you'll need to do before you decide if you want to reel him in.

MEET HIM

▸ Talk about the world. "The [subway / drive over] was crazy tonight. Do you know if there was an accident?" "Isn't this weather [great / awful / strange / apocalyptic]?"

▸ Ask him a question about your surroundings. "Do you know where to find the [drinks / ice / bathroom]?" "Do you know whose artwork this is?" "Have you been here before?" "I'm looking for a drinking glass."

▸ Ask where he's from—or better yet, pretend you can guess where he's from and get it wrong (with a big smile). "Can I ask you a question? I think I can tell where you're from. It's got to be…Uzbekistan!" Alternatively, try the same tactic with his line of work. Always guess that he is a brave, brave fireman.

START A CONVERSATION: SITUATIONAL OPENERS

▸ Exchange names. Feel free to reinvent your last name as "Delicious."

▸ Ask him about himself in relation to where you are. "Are you a friend of the [hostess / performer / bartender]?" "Who do you know here? How did you meet?" "What do you think of [this place / the artwork / the show / the song that's playing]?"

▸ Comment on a noteworthy or unusual item in your surroundings. (But stay away from negative openers; see the "Eject Button" section in chapter 8 for techniques that use negative lines.) "Have you seen the stereo? It's like those huge computers in old sci-fi movies! Number One: engage the disco, stat!" "That houseplant is out of control—I'd be worried I'd wake up in its mouth!" "Isn't this sculpture beautiful? I think it's hand-carved."

▸ Talk about the reason you're there. "How long have you been a fan of Marilyn Manson?" "This is one of my favorite galleries. Do you have a favorite?" "The parties here are always a blast. Have you been here before?" "I've been here a million times but I don't know the history. Do you know anything about it?" (Alternate: "Didn't this Starbucks used to be a mortuary?")

▸ *Absolutely* ask questions you already know the answer to. Ask what time it is, where the snacks are, if the drinks are any good (hide your cocktail), what the weather was like in the city today, etc.

▸ Be humorously contrary; look for humor in your situation and humor in what he says to you. For instance, if it's 100 degrees in the room, ask jokingly if you can borrow a coat.

▸ Encourage him to open up, and agree with him when he shares something personal with you. Give him windows in the conversation to show his personality. And avoid topics like exes, your own sex life (unless you know he's midnight snack material), and mean gossip.

▸ Don't forget to compliment him on something. Say that he's funny (but only if he really is, unless you want to hear fart jokes all night). Tell him he's interesting. Compliment his appearance: his clothing or style, his watch or shoes, his braces, or his toupee. Hey, you never know.

▸ Ask him where his girlfriend is; this will give you a lot of information right away. If he says, "Standing right next to you," flip to chapter 8, Miss Titanic: Avoid a Flirting Disaster, as fast as you can.

Flirt Hacks: Flirting Online

Online flirting can free us up in surprising ways. Self-consciousness can make us nervous and tense, and the relative anonymity of web communications like email, text messaging, instant messaging, and Twitter @ replies and direct messages allows us to flirt in ways we may never try in person. When online, the social restrictions of talking to someone in person are lifted. We tend to say and do things we ordinarily wouldn't when face-to-face because the Internet feels like another world.

It's also easier to say what you mean because you can think about it beforehand, and you can more easily find someone with shared interests. Face-to-face, it's tough to edit what you say in the heat of the moment, but online you usually get a chance (or two) to reread what you wrote before you hit Send. With less pressure, some girls feel that they can be themselves more than in a bar or party situation. Flirting online relies heavily on brainpower and wit, and this is where you'll get a chance to show off those qualities in more ways than you can when first meeting a guy in person.

Online flirting isn't always what it seems, since you're missing many of flirting's important body messages and social cues. Often, we form our opinions based on facial expressions and body movements, so it's a bit tougher to read between the lines accurately when you're flirting in text. Misrepresentation is a big issue, and sending clear messages is a major concern—knowing the guy you're flirting with is on the level. Interestingly, it also gives you a chance to be completely honest about yourself or your opinion of others without having to deal with the social fallout of saying something potentially uncomfortable in person.

Anonymous online flirting can be a total ego boost that leads to nothing more than making you feel good for the rest of the day. Or it can lead further into online dating, phone dating, and possibly even the real-life thing. For many people, online flirting is a fun supplement, a layer of naughty tension added to an exciting real-life situation. The important thing, if you're flirting with a guy you just met online, is to decide early in the conversation whether you're flirting for fun and games, or maybe for something more.

If you're flirting with a man you don't know, follow basic safety rules: never give him your real name or email address, your location, or any identifying details. It's a good idea to stay safe with your online encounters by using an anonymous email address to give out to casual and unfamiliar flirt partners. Also, be sure to learn as much as possible about who you're flirting with (use your Google-fu) to avoid chatting up your boss's brother-in-law.

SOCIAL MEDIA, TWITTER, AND INSTANT MESSAGING FLIRTING TIPS

▸ Start simple: comment on something he posted or Tweeted to get noticed. Ask him a question directly, or point him to a link that you think adds to his conversation.

▸ Be sure to acknowledge the thread of conversation and especially what he is saying.

▸ Always use his screen name as you would his real name if you were meeting in person.

▸ If the guy you're flirting with is interested in you, be courteous to the others in the social media "room" (meaning everyone else who can see it happening) and take your flirting to a private place such as direct messages (DM), instant messages (IM), or email.

▸ Give him three chances to be shy, then take it as a sign of disinterest and move along.

▸ Be creative. Refer to something you've noticed in his profile or on whatever website he links to in his "about" area; cross-reference randomly to one of his "likes" in his profile or something he mentions; or expand on a topic (a band, a movie, a TV show) he mentions and introduce something about it he might not know—or something new related to something he likes. People usually gravitate to those who help them find more of what they like, so run with it!

▸ Don't take anything—I mean *anything*—too seriously or personally. It's really easy to misinterpret tone and meaning online.

▸ Whatever you do, be sure not to overuse "LOL." Once or twice is enough, and use only when genuine.

▸ Follow your instincts with red flags: if you find out he's a musician living off credit cards and you wonder if his "roomie" might be his girlfriend, toss that fish back in the sea.

▸ Be absolutely clear about your interest, feelings, and goals. It's impossible to read between the lines in a chat room, and subtlety and ambiguity will get you nowhere.

EMAIL FLIRTING TIPS

▸ If you're in a casual flirtation with someone, it's perfectly acceptable to send him an email that simply reads "Hi!"

▸ Keep it short and sweet; don't tell your life story. Don't overuse emoticons such as :) and ;) and : P.

▸ Try to give an honest impression of who you are but keep it light and fun at all times. "Too intense" isn't a flirting skill.

▸ How long do you wait to reply? At first, within an hour is fine, or you can leave him hanging for a day—but no longer unless you have a good excuse.

▸ Even if you're really excited, only check your email once an hour.

▸ Don't hit Send if you're not sure about something you wrote, or if you're upset.

▸ Find out what he's interested in, and find an excuse to email him about it.

▸ Don't email again until you get a reply, unless it's playfully urgent.

▸ If you want to make it easy for him to respond, ask clear questions that you know are easy for him to respond to. "What did you have for lunch?" is much easier during the workday than "Did you ever feel lonely as a child?"

▸ Be careful if either of you might be using work computers. It is perfectly legal for a company to read and keep employees' email correspondence, even if it is not work-related.

▸ Make replies easy for your reader: use the Reply button, which will quote what they wrote. (Quoted lines are usually preceded with the [<] symbol; some programs use the pipe [|].) Cut out any of the text that isn't directly relevant to what you are responding to. This keeps him from having to sift through a huge quote or scroll down a lengthy email to figure out what part you are responding to.

▸ Examine what he writes for passion and feeling, or at least humor. In your reply, try to describe something that speaks to that passion, feeling, or humor.

▸ If you start asking each other personal questions about feelings and experiences that have meaning, find out where the personal meanings lie in his daily life. "Do you like what you do for a living?" Also ask the same questions he asks in return.

▸ Be suspicious of questions that seem too personal, or have an agenda, or make you feel uncomfortable. Use your intuition at all times in cyberdating.

▸ If it's not clear what someone's saying, ask for clarification.

▸ If you don't get replies from two emails in a row, move him to the bottom of your priority list.

5 | EASY TRICKS TO BEING A TEMPTING TREAT

You don't need anyone's permission to get what you want. And it doesn't mean you're a brat if you want it *right now*—it means you are a super-sexy, wanton brat and you deserve to get what you want, because you're worth it. Don't worry! Craving instant gratification means that you're not sleepwalking through life in your old tatty slippers and boring old pj's—no, you are strutting seductively through the party in your finest sexy nightie, getting the attention you deserve, and having the time of your life. Demand instant satisfaction with all your flirting encounters, and you'll get results.

Flirting is the number one way to get what you want, whether it's a drink, lusty attention, a super-charged one-nighter, making new friends, finding "the one," learning the whereabouts of Batman's cave, or an offer from Don Draper. To hone your flirting powers to their finest, you'll want to learn techniques that can communicate exactly what you want in five minutes or less. Opening lines and conversation starters are one thing, but how you say them and the way your voice sounds can mean the difference between wanting—and getting.

Sound Sexy

Let's step into the "Wayback Machine" for a minute, back to Hollywood's roaring 1920s, when women were sexy sirens and men were dashing cads. One of the biggest starlets to grace the silent screen was adorable Clara Bow, who was known as the "It" Girl. She was idolized by legions of fans as representing jazz modernity, fierce feminine independence, and most of all, sexual freedom. For women, she was the girl to become, and for men, well, she was the girl to be with. Clara's reign of starring roles came to a shrill end when movies added sound as a layer to the action. The minute she opened her mouth for a screen test, cast and crew ducked for cover as her squeaky, grating tone and untempered Brooklyn accent came amplified through the microphones. Sadly, her voice was untrained, and the mystique of the girl who played a jazz babydoll, Mafia gun moll, and even a Klondike bride was over the minute she opened her mouth.

Each time you open your mouth to that foxy boy is your own private screen test. A little voice prep goes a long way. Even if you don't end up starring in each other's movie, fine-tuning your voice to make a sexy impression might have you (at least) starring in his personal movies later, if you know what I mean.

Find your sexiest voice. Yes, that means you need to listen to yourself, whether that means listening to your outgoing message, reading a food label into a digital recorder, or drinking five Fuzzy Navels and singing recorded karaoke to a roomful of coworkers. Record it, and listen. Get over your inner critic for a minute and listen objectively. Is it high, nervous, tinny? Low, fast, or quiet? Listen to someone whose voice you find sexy, and make notes on how you'll adjust it to find a sexy conversational tone. Record it again, and listen to see if your adjustments work.

Some people have a difficult time hearing their own voice. You might find that trying a few voice exercises gives your voice a sexier and more resonant sound. Practice speaking not from your throat, but from the center of your chest, and pushing the air out from your stomach. Stretch the muscles in your jaw, lips, and tongue to relax your face. Learn to speak softly by lowering your volume (loudness) and pitch (aim for lower notes), but play with resonance. Try a sentence in a low whisper, deeper than your normal voice. Then try it louder, still a bit deeper. Next, hum, keeping your mouth closed. Now speak the sentence in your low whisper, but with the same resonance as the hum. You'll use these different techniques to find the sexy voice that works best for you, and also to gauge volume over music, to sync up with your conversation partner's volume, and match his rhythm as well.

In the moment of *le flirt*, you'll talk in an unrushed tempo in your low, sexy voice, but you'll keep your words clear. Avoid the mistake of sounding too "breathy" in an attempt to be sexy. The three keys are low, slow, and clear. Match the tone, pacing, and rhythm of what he says, and you'll tune right into his interest, feeding the fire with gas. Ask him a few questions, and match his response in timing, volume, and urgency.

What's important is to be as clear as possible in pronunciation and content. Slow down your descriptions; don't rush anything. If you're worried about saying aggressive or forward things out loud because it's something new for you, or you aren't used to saying certain words, find some private time, make a list of words or challenging phrases you think will be weird to say, and say them. Out loud, over and over. Do it in front of a mirror. You'll smile and laugh at first, and it's okay to smile and laugh when you do it in person.

What matters is that you say anything at all, and your desire to connect with him says you *mean* it.

If you still think flirting with words and your voice sounds silly, don't worry. When you say it to him in person, it'll sound plenty sexy.

SAY IT, DON'T SPRAY IT

Want to get lucky when you open your mouth? Follow these guidelines:

▸ No matter how exotic you think the British are, never talk with a mouthful of celery spears.

▸ There is such a thing as overkill. Remember Drew Barrymore in *Poison Ivy*?

▸ Lots of people are grossed out by lipstick rings on drinking glasses, but don't fix the problem by fellating your finger in public. Blot, blot, blot.

▸ If it's so funny that milk comes out your nose or air escapes from your posterior, laugh like a maniac and consider it a test of his resilience. If he fails, he dies.

▸ When a guy is so sexy he makes your mouth water, wait until the flood subsides to find out if he tastes like chicken—say it, don't spray it.

▸ If you do spray, lift a palm to the heavens and ask if it's starting to rain.

▸ In a room that's too loud, be prepared to write messages on anything handy; napkins, business cards, parking tickets, panty liners, and tampon wrappers are all fair game. Shouting in a guy's ear will make him want to flee.

Use Your Powers of Hypnosis

When you're on the prowl, sometimes you practically need to become a one-woman show. Since you can't use tricks like an ancient gypsy love spell on every possibility who looks good in pants (only a select few), you'll want to cultivate your powers of hypnosis. No, not like one of those tapes you listen to while you're asleep that grants you the power to "make any man your slave," though darn close, this type of hypnosis comes from using a few speaking techniques to keep him entertained—or even hanging on your every word.

To lure him in close enough to see if he's worthy, you'll need to make him listen to you. If leading the conversation and keeping people's attention is a foreign concept or if you're a bit shy, cheat—copy the techniques of the pros. Why? Because you can have great lines, a sexy walk, and everything else, but it's all about the delivery, baby.

Next time you're in a crowded atmosphere, spy on a small group of people where one person is the center of attention. Join or stand near the group and study the storyteller closely. Watch how he talks to the group and note whether he focuses on one person in particular. Examine her body language, stance, hand movements, facial expressions, and the movements of her eyes. If you can hear the conversation, check the tone, the topic, how he reacts to others, and figure out what he does that you think works. Discard anything you don't like about her communication with the group. Take note if she seems to be flirting with one person more than another, and decide whether it's working or not, and why.

A good speaker will stand so that his or her body is "open" to everyone listening, especially toward one person in particular. Even if you are not interested in flirting with anyone in your group, focus your open stance toward one of your listeners, or right between two of them. Have your feet apart, toes facing out, and keep your arms uncrossed. Use your hands to illustrate your points and to help you tell a story. Hands are excellent tools to conduct your listener's attention, and you can direct focus to yourself by making finger gestures that mimic pinching, with thumb and forefingers, as if picking up a pen.

Your arm and hand gestures can be subtle and waist-high, or a bit more flamboyant, remaining between your waist and shoulders. Avoid flapping your arms and movements that could send an elbow into an unsuspecting boob (literal or figurative). Outlandish gestures just wind up looking dorky, drunk, or hysterical.

To suggest directness, try to keep your head tilted down slightly as you speak. Keep eye contact, but mix it up. If you're in a group, look at everyone in a pattern that begins and ends with the same person, alternating for breaks when people make jokes or if the conversation moves to another speaker. If you're one-on-one, keep your eye contact consistent while speaking, but take 5-to-10-second visual breaks to let your listener look at other parts of you.

IF HE'S INTERESTED

But is he even listening to your incredible story about saving the kittens from the burning building? When he's really listening, he will show it by:

▸ Making "keep going" gestures, including smiles, nods, little "mmh" noises that punctuate the breaks in your conversation, or small prompts such as "Really?" "What!" "Uh-huh" and "Tell it, girlfriend."

▸ Listening with his body, leaning forward, widening his eyes, and nodding along with positive things you say.

▸ Looking animated.

▸ Asking questions.

▸ Looking at you most of the time you're talking.

▸ Giving you lots of smiles.

IF HE'S LOST INTEREST

If it's time for him to change the channel and flirt with someone else, your nonlistener will show disinterest by:

- Finishing your sentences. (Plus, it's just darn rude. Next!)

- Fidgeting his legs and feet.

- Excessive fiddling with his stuff or person, toying with buttons, digging through his pockets, doodling, and so on.

- Answering his cell phone. (Ugh. This guy is fired as a flirtee!)

- Nodding or making prompting comments at the wrong times.

- Slouching and crossing his arms.

- Making eye contact less than 50 percent of the time.

While the above guidelines are handy for assessing a successful flirting encounter, it just so happens that quite a few of us tend to be attracted to members of the herd some might consider shy, introverted, geeky, or nerdy—even socially dysfunctional mad-scientist types. These subsets of the species are tougher to read. He could be going out of his mind to get you alone and hanging on your every word, but his excitement translates into obsessively folding a napkin until it disintegrates or answering your queries with nervous little grunts.

These special creatures are worth experimenting with. Change the topic. Ask about his life. Change your tone and deepen your voice slightly. Slow your speech down a notch or two, and lower your volume a tiny bit. Or speed up the pace and don't be afraid to make silly jokes. Shy guys tend to be smarter than the rest and will appreciate your willingness to make fun of yourself, and everyone else.

Speed Flirting

———

Let's be honest. For the goal oriented, flirting is shopping. And when you're out shopping, you want the best selection, best prices and the best-put-together package you can find. Be discriminating, be finicky. Most of all, be a smart shopper. Compare and size up the merchandise—and don't waste too much time trying to make an attractive pair of uncomfortable shoes fit.

Eliminate the guessing game of flirting for 20 minutes only to learn that he charges by the hour. There are ways you can find out if he's worth the effort fairly quickly, so you won't waste your valuable flirting time on a rentboy (unless you're shopping for a stud-for-hire, but that's a topic for a different book). It's in your best interest to find out as soon as possible if he's out for a one-night stand or something more; then you can decide what *you* want. The amount of time it takes to suss out a potential playmate is only around 10 minutes. It sounds crafty, but don't you think being a bit sly makes the chase more fun?

TEN MINUTES AND COUNTING:

▸ Check him out and make your approach. Still look good to you, or are you getting a red flag about anything? Listen to your intuition.

▸ Decide whether you'll use a persona, and then make the first move. "Hi, I'm Christina—Christina Hendricks. What's that you're drinking?"

▸ Ask four questions: what is his favorite movie or TV show?, what did he have for dinner?, who does he live with?, and what does he do for a living? A bonus question: what does he think of "intimate shaving"? Points are added if you're in a movie star persona and he lists all "your" movies. The conversation ends if he still lives with Mom and Dad.

▸ As he answers, size him up as if he were marrying your best friend. Ask yourself: Are those lips kissable? Would his neck smell good? Is he talking with his mouth full? Would your naked bodies rub together well? Could I laugh at his farts? Would your best friend ever forgive you?

▸ Judge him harshly. If he passes, you can judge him lightly and silently later.

▸ If you like him, get his phone number or email address. Don't give him yours.

▸ Excuse yourself, and leave the conversation.

Ding! You're done. Is he? Be extra clever and try to rack up four or five speed-flirting sessions a night.

6 | READY-TO-WEAR SEDUCTION

Now it's time to deal with some of the most difficult decisions in your flirt career—what will you wear? How will you compose yourself? What gets you in the right attitude to strut your stuff and get your groove on? As shallow as it sounds, people will instantly judge you as harshly as an Olympic ice skater in Spandex ruffles, deciding how hot, sexy, and delicious you look and carry yourself at any given moment. Show them you are dishy. Prove your high scores for couture with every step. Make them see that you have the best routine and the wicked moves that deserve a gold medal for flirting. Maximize your flirt style and he'll be eating out of your hand—or sipping champagne from your stiletto, as you please.

You'll need to look good while you're being bad, no matter whether you're sweetly naughty or devastatingly seductive. Take the flirt style test in chapter 1 to see what motivates your flirt style; then refer to the following choices to help your most important decisions become critical keys to your flirting success.

Flirting with Style: Your Seduction Persona

Let your inner Sweetheart, Diva, Femme Fatale, or Ruler of All Mankind guide the way. Think you may be a little of each? Pick and choose to make a style all your own.

SWEETHEART CHIC

Attract the bees to your honey with blossoms: no matter what you wear, your best accessories are your smile, a knowing look, and easy laughter. To make the most of your Sweetheart status, glean useful tips by reading up on flirty stances and sexy walking. You may identify most with the sexy librarian icon. If so, the area where you most need polish is getting noticed (chapter 2), and you'll get the most from dance or burlesque classes.

THE LOOK: Casual and comfortable, sexy and loose summer clothes, flirty and fun, but you seldom go overboard with trends or sexually revealing outfits. Dressing sexy means adding a few extra touches such as a little makeup or gloss, touchable hair, unbuttoning the top buttons of your shirt, or slipping into something made of soft fabrics or with tactile, visually appealing textures. For you, surface sexiness means communicating a touchable sensuality—and it works.

THE ATTITUDE: Melts in your mouth, not in your hands.

CONFIDENCE CURE: Practice the body language techniques in chapter 2. Fake it till you make it.

THE APPROACH: Smooth as butter, baby. Smile sweet as pie at your flirt target *du jour* and take your time on the approach. Stay in his line of sight, but tease and move in slow. You reel him in, hook line and sinker, and before he knows it, you're standing right next to him, smiling and ready to say, "Hi."

CONVERSATION STARTER: Simple is the name of the game for you. Say hi, and comment on objects that are in front of you; the party, his jacket, the furniture, the artwork, or the artist passed out under the table.

IDEAL FLIRT CONDITIONS: Mild to moderate. Daytime parties, casual cocktail gatherings, weddings, art galleries, cafés, dinner parties, bookstores, industry or business-related meet-ups, conferences, reunions, events like organizational parties, on vacation, and in classrooms.

LAUNCH PAD CHECKLIST: Lip gloss, rose-colored glasses.

SWEETHEART ALIAS NAME GENERATOR: Take the name of your favorite childhood toy and combine it with your favorite childhood dessert. For instance, you might introduce yourself as Barbie Double Scoop, Easy Bake Shortcake, or Kitten Otter Pop.

DIVA VOGUE

Ready to strike the right pose, shake your booty on the dance floor, or look sassy reeling in the bohunk of the day? DivaGrrl, in this book you get the most from tips about eye contact and facial expression. Seek out Diva flirting fix-its in your conversation starters and topics—this is where your come-on needs a little TLC. Get your chit-chat in gear, and you're set.

THE LOOK: Skin is always in, and while you like to feel comfortable, you don't have that sexy feeling unless you've got a little flesh on display. Cleavage, midriff, legs: even if you're wearing a turtleneck and slacks, you'll excel if your feet and ankles send sexual signals in a pair of flirty sandals.

THE ATTITUDE: Slippery when wet.

CONFIDENCE CURE: The life of the party is sometimes the biggest dork. When you do something especially geeky, show 'em your pearly whites and take a big bow. Read more about dorking out with style in chapter 2.

THE APPROACH: Direct but cute. You want him to know it's a come-on, but you aren't going to suddenly turn into *Single White Female*. Flirt while dancing, cock your head and smile as if you're about to laugh, and bounce right up to the boys that interest you. Your humor for life and your outward charm are infectious.

CONVERSATION STARTER: You're not afraid to make a joke to get the juices flowing—a good joke, a bad joke, it's all fun and games. Be contrary and silly about your surroundings, and it's a natural fit. "Any Iron Maiden in this playlist?"

IDEAL FLIRT CONDITIONS: Hot and steamy. Bars, clubs, parties (especially theme parties), beaches, girls' night out, cafés, movie screenings, after-hours bashes, and even places where you don't feel you fit in. Your energetic style makes you stand out in a sedate crowd.

LAUNCH PAD CHECKLIST: A sexy scent (perfume, moisturizer, body butter) and dancing shoes.

DIVA ALIAS NAME GENERATOR: A word you'd use to describe a hot prospect, combined with your favorite ice cream flavor. By night, you are Dishy Butterscotch, Sweet Peppermint, Foxy Nut Crunch or Tasty Mocha Fudge.

FEMME FATALE BOMBSHELL

Get ready, Bombshell, because when you enter a room, all eyes are on you and all jaws hit the floor like spent shells from a smoking gun. You've got the walk down and the smoldering gaze to back it up; delivering an opening line is as easy for you as taking candy from a baby boy—or letting him know that *you're* the candy he needs. Polish up your pout and make your flirting techniques shine by learning the tips and tricks for what to do once you're in place and the conversation's flowing. You need the most help with staying put and keeping your body language in line. Focus on hands, arms, legs, and feet, and using them to your utmost advantage. The boys'll be singing your name from behind bars in no time.

THE LOOK: Retro flair and high style is the name of the game. You wear a "look" well, and become absolutely magnetic when you're all put together. Hair done up sexy and stylish, carefully selected accessories (in bracelets *and* crime), and clothing that knows when to be both flatteringly tight and loose to complement your curves. Fifties retro, sixties mod, seventies glam, eighties go-go, or chic twists on the classic styles amp up your sex appeal. No matter what you wear, your sexy underwear is your secret weapon.

THE ATTITUDE: Dangerous curves.

CONFIDENCE CURE: Blame others for your agony, and drown your sorrows in the arms of a tall, cool drink of handsome stranger. (More confidence cures in chapter 2.)

THE APPROACH: You make your plan according to what puts you at an advantage. You like to size up the situation and proceed with caution thrown to the wind. You can be demure or bold or even play damsel in distress, depending on which way the wind's blowing. You play whatever part you think will turn him on the most.

CONVERSATION STARTER: A well-timed accident or a blatant "Come here often?" are both humorous and devilish enough to get the party started. Employ any opener that starts your encounter off as a fun game.

IDEAL FLIRT CONDITIONS: Heat wave, all the way. Anything that gets you close and personal will be where you can work your magic: an intimate corner of a pub, a booth, a quiet dinner party, interrogation room, scene of the crime, art gatherings, private parties, cocktail affairs, or boardroom affairs.

LAUNCH PAD CHECKLIST: A compact mirror for omni-directional flirting, and super-sexy underwear.

FEMME FATALE ALIAS NAME GENERATOR: Sometimes you need an alibi and sometimes you just need to be someone else. Combine your favorite flower with your favorite lingerie fabric to become Rose Velour, Jasmine Velvet, Iris Silk, or Lily Lace.

RULER OF ALL MANKIND SEDUCTRESS

Men: they're what's for dinner. Style, panache and a touch of super-villainess insanity make you the most magnetic woman in the room, whether you're arriving in an explosion of smoke, gliding in on the backs of your henchmen, or simply sitting on your mechanical throne stroking your fluffy white cat. Who cares if you come on too strong if you're the one holding the ray gun? Making an entrance, delivering openers, and flaunting your body language are all part of

117

your character; the only spot you need to perfect is the switch—when things don't go as planned, you get cranky. Don't seek vengeance, instead, read chapter 8.

THE LOOK: Sinister and sexy is the name of the game. Seduce with a skintight catsuit and let your feminine wiles do the rest until your butt is firmly planted on that padded throne. Subtle is not necessary; instead, you find that costumes suited to your unnatural abilities work best. Have a bad lab accident with rose fertilizer chemicals that gave you superpowers? The natural answer is red latex with thorny accessories, of course. Able to control the weather since birth and have major jealousy issues? Keep that hair long and lustrous, and any low-cut, flowing garments will do.

THE ATTITUDE: When I'm bad, I'm better.

CONFIDENCE CURE: Pretend you are foreign and "ask" attractive targets for information, such as where the drinks are, where the foreign dignitaries hide the secret documents, and so on. Summon your inner Natasha from *Rocky and Bullwinkle*. Find more confidence cures in chapter 2.

THE APPROACH: Bold is putting it lightly, though you do enjoy playing cat-and-mouse with your male prey. Leading the forces of good on a wild-goose chase that leads back to you is a good start; performing a daring public criminal stunt is another way you like to get your flirt on.

CONVERSATION STARTER: With good guys, making it a challenge to catch you is a surefire way to garner interest, while bad boys are a bit trickier and like to think they can beat you to the punch. Make a game between the two of you out of stealing that famous diamond from the museum, and see how intimate you become.

IDEAL FLIRT CONDITIONS: Your affections are like a storm. They rage in and subside just as quickly. Dramatic conditions suit you best: castles, underground labs, back rooms, rooftops, evil lairs, telemarketing conferences, haunted woods, abandoned shacks, private islands, penthouse suites, ice fortresses, and secret hideouts.

LAUNCH PAD CHECKLIST: Daytime disguise in your purse or utility belt, secret weapon, body glitter.

RULER OF ALL MANKIND ALIAS NAME GENERATOR: This is where you can get really creative. One name or two, it's your call, but make it descriptive, memorable, and catchy—above all, it has to remind that bad boy what your most fearful powers are. And be feminine. Contradictions are wonderful, such as combining a quality of good with an evil-sounding name, such as Hope Bloodspill, Ophelia Christian, Faith Borden or Charity Blackheart. Or you can combine your favorite color with a last name made up of your favorite thing and your favorite nefarious activity. This conjures up wonderfully Gothic names like Ruby Nightshriek, Violet Blackdirge, Emerald Painsmoke and Sage Soulstealer.

Wicked Flirt Checklist

———

Bad girl, good girl—it's an endless cycle. Now you're ready to join the party. Don't leave the house without your utility belt, your magic lasso, and your wicked bag of shiny new flirting tricks. Check the boxes below before you enter a room, or cut out the list and keep it handy as a cheat sheet. Make notes wherever necessary—flirting legends all have lists on their refrigerators, too.

❏ Flirt Mode (chapter 2): head up, shoulders back; slow down; pause before you start.

❏ Pussycat Walk (chapter 2): walk the line, arms straight, shoulders in motion.

❏ Silent seductions: eyes, smile, hands, arms, feet (chapter 3).

❏ Positioning and signaling (chapter 3).

- ❏ The SIS test (chapter 4).

- ❏ Conversation starters / opening lines (chapter 4).

- ❏ To-do list for names of flirt targets.

- ❏ Ready bedpost for new notches.

7 | GIRL ON THE PROWL

You're ready to flirt. All you need is an invitation to cut loose. The minute you see that sexy dish, all bets are off, and with a toss of the hair, straightening of the shoulders, and a twinkle in your eye, you're ready to reel him in. That is, if he's interested. How do you know if he wants to play?

Flirt, Friend, or Pass: Does He Want Me?

Every time you turn on the flirt vibes, you become the star of your own totally fabulous movie, starring you.

The camera moves in for a seductive close-up as your eyes scan the room looking for fun. You make a mental list: there's boy number one, two, three—then line 'em up and knock 'em down. But how do you know your approach will be welcome, let alone successful?

Don't mistake a piece of fuzz caught in his eye for that "come hither" wink: look for the physical clues that reveal his interest, whether he knows it or not. You know from reading the previous chapters how to physically entice, intrigue, and let your man-target know you're game, but reading those sexy signs in reverse might take a little practice. In addition, there are other unconscious physical signs he'll exhibit when he finds someone attractive, and you'll want to check that you've seen at least three attraction-positive physical or facial expressions before you even say hi.

MIRROR, MIRROR: Be keenly aware of your flirty stance, body movements, gestures, and facial expressions. When someone begins to subtly imitate you, they're locked into you and are feeling the pull of attraction. Watch for things he'll do that copy you—legs crossed or uncrossed, positions of hands and arms, shoulders squared to face you directly, and of course, mirrored facial expressions such as eye contact, smiling, and sipping his drink when you sip yours.

EYE'VE GOT TO HAVE YOU: Prolonged eye contact is like firing a starting gun to let the races begin, and repeated eye contact is like having the light change from red to green. If you catch him checking you out, bust him with a smile that says "Gotcha!" and flirt shamelessly, enjoying every moment. One careless glance isn't enough, but if there is a second look, stay tuned to see what his body tells you next. Sometimes the second look lingers for a second, and this can be considered an engraved invitation to flirt freely. If his eye contact is fleeting and you can't tell if it's accidental, wait to see if it happens more than three times, and look for a secondary physical clue just to be sure.

HOT LIPS: When people are tense or uninterested, they keep their lips clamped together. But when someone's hormones click from "off" to "on" in that moment of animal attraction, their lips part slightly, invitingly. Licking lips, touching lips with a finger or straw, or touching a glass for a moment longer than needed before taking a sip can indicate his aroused interest.

FACE-OFF: Watch his entire face for further signs of interest. People feeling attraction toward you will relax their faces, softening their eyes and their smile. Small movements such as subtly raised eyebrows or a half-smile give away curiosity. A barely noticeable flaring of the nostrils reveals interest.

IT'S ALL ABOUT ME: Actually, it is all about you. But someone who is open to a few rounds of flirting will try to grab your attention somehow, in ways that range from subtle and unconscious to overt and flashy. Active listening is always a good sign. He might act more flirtatious toward you than others. Obvious signs aside, little movements that draw attention to his body can be giveaways, such as adjusting clothing, smoothing hair, stroking facial stubble, putting a hand on the chest, fixing a button or snap, or smoothing out wrinkles. Some guys will stand to face you directly even while talking to others, and another clue is when he faces you with both hands on his hips. Attention-grabbers who still want to play it safe will find an excuse to stand near you, yet not quite face you—and that's right when the ball lands in your court. A bonus is when his friends pay attention to you when he has left the room—a sign that he's talked positively about you to his friends.

YOU ARE THE HUNTRESS

You don't need an engraved invite delivered on a silver platter, but it's not exactly like potential flirt targets are walking by wearing little signs around their necks that say "Come get me!" or flashing secret hand signals. No, these wily beasts camouflage themselves well—in crowds, in cityscapes, and anywhere else you might expect "average Joes" to gather. Well, you may never know when or where one will appear, but when he does, he'll be easy to recognize once you learn the many styles and models of the receptive flirtee.

A Guide to Men in the Wild

—

ART GUY

He has no job, he comes from money, and yet he runs from money—but the romantic allure of the passionate, troubled artist and magnetic attraction to the weight of the world on his sexy shoulders is undeniable. Found lurking at art shows, openings, events, fund-raisers (for himself and friends), in school or studio, Art Guy digs a good conversation, especially if it's about him or deconstructing someone else's work. These creatures hover at watering holes where free wine and cheese are readily available, and flirting with him is a snap if you grab his attention with questions or comments about the food / art. Alter ego: Rock Star.

HE'S SIZING YOU UP AS A POSSIBLE LIFE DRAWING MODEL WHEN: He squares his shoulders toward you, focuses his burning, artful gaze deep into your eyes, and tells you his reason for living / financial woes.

BOHUNK

Sometimes also known as "Bad Boy" or "Tough Guy," this irresistible number spells "trouble" and "fun" with the same letters—usually because spelling is low on his list of skills. This model is eye candy, pure and simple, and promises a rough and randy roll in the hay. Competition might be stiff, but you'll have the upper hand when you use your physical flirting skills: gently invade his space with a soft smile, and lead his eyes with your hands.

HE'S GOT YOU IN HIS SIGHTS WHEN: His physical response mirrors yours, and he stands or sits facing you completely.

CRIMINAL MASTERMIND

This guy will make you feel like you can rule the world together—and if his evil plan comes to pass, you will. Usually found in underground secret lairs, laboratories, floating ocean fortresses, and marketing seminars, the Criminal Mastermind exudes power and kinky sexuality that few can resist. Once you get close, he'll eat out of the palm of your hand and tell you how to use the death ray, though the approach is seldom simple. Be direct, with constant, piercing eye contact and closed-lipped smiles, and bring him a hero to torture to get the conversation started. Or wear white, pretend to be a "good girl," and agree to surrender and be his sexy captive, ASAP.

HE WANTS YOU TO HELP HIM DESTROY THE FORCES OF GOOD WHEN: He asks you which side you're on, then lets you hold and pet the fluffy white cat wearing really sexy outfits bearing his evil emblem.

LADYKILLER PICKUP ARTIST (OR DOUCHEBAG)

It's as if he knows everyone is looking at him—and maybe so, because Mr. Ladykiller's smarmyness surrounds him like Pig Pen's dust cloud. Maybe in his boyish past he might have been socially awkward, but now he's Mr. Smooth, and you'll notice him when he eyes you up and down like prime sirloin at the supermarket. You're the queen of the universe when he thinks you're fair game, but he loves himself most of all. Does he tell you that your teeth are crooked while trying to get in your panties? Does he point out something you're unhappy about and then ask you if you're really happy—while trying to get in your panties? The Douchebag or Ladykiller Pickup Artist likes to trick girls into the sack, which is fine if you're looking for a sack of *something*. This kind can be fun for flings and one-nighters because they're high energy and no-strings, but don't expect anything afterward, and know that you're the one paying for your own drinks.

YOU KNOW IT'S FLIRTING OPEN SEASON WHEN: You've got a pulse.

MR. NONFAT HALF-CAF

Don't you just want to find out what's in those Dockers? A raging stallion, that's what. Every yuppie is a sexual animal in disguise, waiting to be uncorked like a bottle of foamy champagne, and with a few precise flirting techniques, it's playtime at the zoo in no time. Mr. Nonfat presents as superficial, so your confidence and physical presentation are important—walk, stand,

and sit with all your sexy confidence skills. This animal can smell sexual tension from a mile away (yet seldom shows it), so lure him in with sexy hands and arms, and then hook him with a soft smile.

HE IS A DEER IN THE HEADLIGHTS WHEN: Prolonged eye contact happens and he gravitates near you, invading your space. If you approach, look for nervous glances, and on first eye contact, say hi.

MYSTERY MAN

Quiet, mysterious, and alluring, this rare bird will either be hiding a powerful intellect and keen observational skills with which he sees all, or casing the joint for burglar alarms and easy escapes later. This one plays hard to get at every turn, and if a dry martini "shaken, not stirred" doesn't loosen him up, and his name isn't "Bond," then you'll need to pull out the big guns to get his guard down for a little *flirt-à-flirt*.

SIDLE UP TO HIM AT THE ROULETTE TABLE WHEN: He's made eye contact with you twice.

ROMANTIC

Dressed with care and wearing at least one item that looks like an old favorite, the Romantic can be spotted by his many creature comforts—comfortable shoes, fashionable drink, and attention to conversation. This one's all about atmosphere, so you'll find him hovering in flattering light, looking for someone to talk with. He won't be standing there with flowers in his hand waiting for you, but you can visualize your forthcoming huge bouquet of long-stemmed red roses while you make eye contact and smile shyly—a big turn-on for Romantics. This kind can make for a great lover, or a fun dating partner.

DON'T PICK OUT RINGS AND CHINA JUST YET—WAIT UNTIL: He responds to your smile with a sweet smile of his own.

TECH GEEK

Geeks and bookworms are the final flirting frontier, and they make a delicious challenge for the seasoned flirt. Getting close to them may tax your most refined hunting skills, but the chase is well worth it when you get these untapped sources of simmering sexual tension to open up. Use every flirting technique at your disposal, and persevere especially when you make it to the conversation stage—don't give up unless he runs away and leaves his pocket protector behind. The Tech Geek may send you mixed physical messages, such as crossed and tense arms, no smile, and hunched shoulders, so pay attention to his eye contact and conversation responses. Do not confuse Tech Geek with Mr. Depression, who makes flirting as exciting as watching paint dry.

HE'S DEFINITELY INTERESTED WHEN: He stops staring at the floor for more than a few seconds and looks in your eyes, his responses to your questions are warm and more than one word, and he asks you a question in response. And when he insists on showing you his awesome gadget, it's actually his phone.

The Truth about a Man's Feet

———

Sizing up your dish of the day takes more than wearing your douchebag decoder ring; you'll need to know if he's worthy before your friends spot the two of you and start texting you about bachelorette party plans. You don't want to reel in what looks like a good catch only to find out that he's been in the "catch and release" loop for a while—or worse, start feeling proud of your bad self for getting a chat-up by the hot guy in the club only to find out he goes by "ManHo" on the pickup artist online message boards.

Well, the old adage about a man and his feet is true: size matters—just not in the way you've heard. The most villainously successful keepers of girl flirt secrets say that you can size a guy up by looking at his shoes. But—big feet do not necessarily mean a big surprise in his boxers. (And the same goes for the myth that a big package means hot sex.) What's essential is the size of his style. In footwear. Everything he doesn't want you to know is right there in plain sight. What he's wearing on his feet can tell you *everything*.

Especially everything about how he's going to treat you. A man's shoes are very personal for him, yet they convey how he sees, respects, and treats things he keeps close to him or cares about. If he doesn't care about his shoes, or how they look to potential mates (even if the mating is short-lived, like under an hour), then you can bet your favorite lipstick he's going to treat you the same way—he'll pick out his ladies the same way as his loafers.

You're at a party or in the club. He's hot. But what's on his feet? When you're out on the hunt, size up a man by his shoe style.

STYLE: Gym shoes

SIZE MATTERS: Baby boy just came from the gym, or he's trying to distract you from his 12-pack belly by pretending he's working on his six-pack, or he's got a great career as a gym…attendant. He gets points for top-shelf brands (style statement), but put him back in the shoebox if they look like the pair he wore on the first day of high school.

STYLE: Crocs, flip-flops, or sandals over socks

SIZE MATTERS: Oh, snap: it's your dad. Or someone else's dad. Next!

STYLE: Combat boots

SIZE MATTERS: He's trying to tell you he's a rebel. Or that the empty chip bags in his room are at least ankle-deep. Unless those boots are shiny and matched with a uniform, he's a rebel without a cause and those boots are made for walking between the art school and the unemployment office. Rebels usually can't afford the next round.

STYLE: Leather / men's couture

SIZE MATTERS: He's successful and cool, worldly and stylish. Glossy cool means he likes to slip in and out *sans* commitment; cool with a worn heel means *he's* a bit of a worn heel.

STYLE: Cowboy boots

SIZE MATTERS: Either a new sheriff is in town or your flirt target wants to have hipster sex like it's 1995 all over again. Well, maybe no one tells Bo Duke how to dress, or no one told him it was time to wear grown-up shoes when he goes out. Put him back in the closet if you don't like being a "little lady."

STYLE: Platforms

SIZE MATTERS: Platforms ranging from Simon Cowell's to RuPaul's mean that he will always dress better than you, even if he doesn't. Pursue him if all the sex you ever want to have is watching *Sex and the City* together.

Reading Signals: Your X-Ray Ray-Bans

———

The difference between what he says and what he really means can mean the difference between successful flirting and making a total dork out of yourself. Unless you're good at working the cute dork angle, learn how to read between the lines. And sometimes, it's almost as if you need a translator.

WHAT HE SAYS: Have you been here before?

WHAT HE REALLY MEANS: Please talk to me.

WHAT HE SAYS: That's a great [dress / skirt / top / bikini].

WHAT HE REALLY MEANS: I want to see what's inside the pretty wrapper. (*And I checked out your butt.*)

WHAT HE SAYS: Can I buy you a drink?

WHAT HE REALLY MEANS: I will buy you something if you will please talk to me.

WHAT HE SAYS: Your makeup is fabulous.

WHAT HE REALLY MEANS: We should shop for makeup together.

WHAT HE SAYS: Friends are more important to me than anything.

WHAT HE REALLY MEANS: This is a one-night deal.

WHAT HE SAYS: I'm really close with my family.

WHAT HE REALLY MEANS: Unless you will be my mommy.

WHAT HE SAYS: I love to work out / I'm a spinning instructor / I'm a triathlete.

WHAT HE REALLY MEANS: I can't get over how beautiful my own body is. Sex will always revolve around my fathomless beauty.

WHAT HE SAYS: I was raised Catholic.

WHAT HE REALLY MEANS: I hope you're into spanking.

WHAT HE SAYS: I love Boston Market.

WHAT HE REALLY MEANS: My bachelor pad is a pigpen.

WHAT HE SAYS: My work always comes first in my life.

WHAT HE REALLY MEANS: I suck in bed.

8 | MISS TITANIC: AVOID A FLIRTING DISASTER

No flirt fatale of any kind will go out for an evening of hunting and bagging boy-babes without encountering a few pitfalls. Competition, duds, interference, mixed messages, and outright mistakes can easily turn a lovely outing into a three-hour tour of duty. Everybody gets rejected, and every gal has a bad experience flirting at some point in her life. But if you never risk the pitfalls, you'll bore yourself to tears with your own life story. Learn when to fix it, when to trash it, how to play slipups to your favor, and how to read between his lines.

How Do You Slay the Competition?

Imagine this scenario: the game is on, he's in your sights, and you're about to approach, open the conversation, and become that shiny thing he's just got to have. Right then, your nemesis walks up and she's in full-on Flirt Mode. What do you do?

Well, you could actually slay her. You are the Queen of this game, and in the land you rule you could just take her out. But in the rest of the world, driving an actual stake through her heart might not be such a good idea, and the hot boy watching you fight to the death over him might not think you look as sexy when you've just turned the competition into a litter pile of smoking ashes. Even if it sounds really satisfying. Better to save your slaying skills for vampires, and learn to dust your competition off like fluff on a jacket.

It happens to the best of us, and I mean the best. Remember that flirting is like any kind of hunting: you should always have a catch-and-release policy. If he's that distracted by her expensive boob job, then you can guess that his make-out skills are about as deep as his personality, and let that one go.

He may have signaled that he's not interested and you missed the red flag. You can tell he has checked out if he's not showing reciprocal signals, or you detect a mood shift (meaning he's changed his mind), or he's playing mind games with you—these can signal an opening for another girl to step in, especially if he wants to play you off another woman to compete for his attention. None of this should ever be taken personally.

HERE ARE SIX TIPS FOR SLAYING THE COMPETITION:

▸ Decide whether he's worth it.

▸ Check to see if he's still interested.

▸ Send four flirt signals and see if he responds to you.

▸ Give her room to look foolish.

▸ Don't stop throwing him smiles.

▸ Select an opportunity to close the deal. (How to close is covered in the next chapter.)

The Interference Test

Imagine that you're flirting shamelessly, having a fun time feeling sexy, in control, perhaps a little out of control in the right ways, making an electric connection with a guy who turns you on. And then, up walks your nemesis. Sexy, confident, chatty, and evil as the day is long, she begins to unravel all your handiwork. What you do next can make or break your success with the object of your desire. It's a sticky situation and it doesn't always pan out, but how you react can sway things in your favor. Take the following quiz to see how your reaction scores:

1. When I realize that someone is competing with me, my first reaction is to:

A. Stand my ground and bemusedly watch her make a fool of herself.

B. Crank up my flirting a notch—she can't touch this!

C. Climb up on the bar and claw her eyes out.

2. If she's using body language that is sexier than mine, or using cleavage or a short skirt as leverage, I:

A. Straighten up, pull back my shoulders, move closer to him, and square off to the competition.

B. Move between them, with my back to the she-bitch.

C. Distract both of them with something across the room, and empty the poison I keep in my ruby-red skull ring into the competition's drink.

3. When in doubt, I channel my inner:

A. Aretha Franklin.

B. Sue Sylvester.

C. Norman Bates.

4. A nice trick to use in situations like this is:

   A. Referring to a shared joke that he and I laughed about earlier.

   B. A thoughtfully spilled drink.

   C. A poison dart.

5. I pump myself up by thinking about lyrics from:

   A. Donna Summer's "I Will Survive."

   B. Rick James's "Super Freak."

   C. "Cruella De Vil," *101 Dalmatians*.

6. If all else fails, I can always:

   A. Move on, and let him suffer fools gladly.

   B. Lean over and ask him to leave with me.

   C. Call forth the forces of darkness to rain terror and suffering upon them both.

7. I visualize:

A. An aura of strength and attraction around me at all times.

B. Crows pecking out her eyes while she's tied to a tree.

C. The enemy trapped in a spider web, shouting for help in her squeaky little voice.

8. I call in reinforcements consisting of:

A. My pals, who make me feel that I belong there and make my flirt target feel included.

B. Drinks, and more drinks.

C. Winged monkeys, undead minions who do my bidding, evil animal companions, or any professional spammers who happen by.

9. To get what I want from the situation, I try to stretch:

A. My courage.

B. My reach for a right hook.

C. My evil laugh into a hideous, shriveling cackle.

10. If I don't succeed, I can always:

A. Chalk one up to experience, and keep flirting!

B. Corner her in the bathroom later and explain that you're carrying his baby / STD / lethal virus for a secret government experiment.

C. Curse her to a life of pain and suffering. (The usual.)

Did you stand your ground and get the prize? Read on to see how you scored.

IF YOU ANSWERED MOSTLY A:

Flirting is a fun and healthy sport for you, something you don't take too seriously. When faced with a challenge, you stand your ground and employ a few sneaky tricks—but only within reason. If someone tries to compete with you, it's easy for you to see how silly it all is, and you hope that your flirtee will see that competition can be fun, or just plain childish. Either way, you know that you're a prize worth winning.

IF YOU ANSWERED MOSTLY B:

Don't mess with Texas! You find competition trifling and it only takes you a second to establish who was there first—and who'll be the last woman standing. Your techniques work most of the time, when they don't scare off your flirt target, and when they work well you are the queen supreme of the flirt scene. And the toughest babe in cell block C.

IF YOU ANSWERED MOSTLY C:

Can't they tell you're the Chosen One? It's tough being a supernatural man-trap and having to devour the souls of those who dare cross you, but your evil life must go on. Once they're both incapacitated and ready for suspension over the pool of hungry sharks, it'll be too late for good-byes, or even "I'm sorry"s. But this is the life of the femme fatale, heartbreaker, wearer of sexy villainess costumes, and destroyer of all that is good and cute.

You're Mistaken—He's Taken

Competition and interference from others is not unusual when you're chatting up someone particularly sexy. But if you discover that you're getting inter-ference because someone else got there first—in a big way, as in, "That's my boyfriend you're flirting with"—then you have some graceful backpedaling to do. There are a few strategies you can use to find out whether this guy is taken before it becomes a court case. You can ask, "So where is your girlfriend tonight?" or "Which one of these ladies is your girl?" This should help you avoid a Titanic-scale disaster.

No matter whether you're a shy girl or a man-eater, if

he's already got someone else's shoes under his bed, the right thing to do is feign surprise and apologize. Make friends by saying, with sincerity, "Oops! I'm sorry. I was flirting where I shouldn't have been. Can I buy you both drinks?" Of course, the couple may or may not be up for "sharing," whether you're in San Francisco or Utah. But you may well find yourself parking your shoes between his and hers, or his and his.

Speaking of San Francisco, it just so happens that a significant majority of the cute, well-dressed, and culturally savvy ones in major urban areas are gay. (Of course, you can count on the opposite being true if you're gay—the cutest one behind the record store counter will turn out to be straight.) So what if you're a straight woman and find yourself barking up the wrong, albeit foxy, tree? No big deal. When he states the obvious—"That's just what my last boyfriend liked! Martinis served in a pint glass!"—state the obvious right back by admitting your oops, followed by a compliment: "Omigod, I was just totally flirting with you. You're so hot—how are you *still* single?" If all goes well, you'll have a new friend instantly and will have access to meeting new people through your new pal. And meeting new people, however they identify sexually, opens up new possibilities while making you look fun, confident and attractive. Cultivate your social networks, and you'll reap positive rewards.

But the best way to avoid hitting an iceberg in a roomful of couples is to look for signs that he's already attached. Hickeys, holding someone else's coat, and a wedding ring are all obvious signs. Don your sexy detective's hat and investigate the signs before you make your approach. Take note of these indicators:

▸ Singles look around the room at everyone, scanning for playmates. He'll look up when new people enter the room; attached people won't.

▸ Look for two drinks on the table in front of him. Could belong to his lover, his friend, or a drunk single Gemini.

▸ Couples don't always act like they're together. Watch to see if he keeps "checking in" with someone via eye contact.

▸ Does it look like he's coyly flirting with someone? Move on.

▸ Holding two plates of snacks? More likely hooked up than really, really hungry.

Eject Button

———

All signs were go, so you started to divide and conquer. But within a few minutes, you know you made a mistake. How do you get out of it? Try these handy tips:

▸ Display the opposite of all the flirty body language signals you've learned in this book: stop smiling, cut off (or avoid) eye contact, slouch, cross your arms, decline his offers.

▸ Tell him you're flattered by his compliments, but just want him to know you're not "on the prowl" right now.

▸ Look bored.

▸ Tell him he just reminded you of this guy you have a crush on.

▸ Pick your teeth with a knife.

▸ Talk about your husband and co-wives.

▸ Tell him you have to sit down because you're so hung over you think you're "going to barf."

▸ Fake an orgasm.

▸ When he asks what you do for a living, say you collect unemployment and watch reruns of reality shows all day.

▸ Tell him how much you hate bathing.

▸ Burp the lyrics to whatever song is playing.

▸ Thrust your pelvis in time with your burps.

▸ Disagree with everything he says.

▸ Ask what his favorite food is, and laugh about how it gives you explosive diarrhea.

EXIT LINES

"Excuse me. Nature calls."

"I [have to get back to / need to check on] my friends."

"I think my parole officer is calling."

"Oops! Did I spill any on you? I'm going to get another one."

"I'm sorry, I need to check my phone. My boyfriend is going to [text / call / meet me]."

Flirting with Disaster

Even the most experienced flirt will find herself in this situation: you sidle up and start chatting, making jokes and flirting, and then—he goes cold. The music stops, the birds stop singing, suddenly your whites aren't as bright. What happened?

When someone stops being interested, or something else is going on altogether, his body language, and sometimes his verbal language, tells you immediately. He will present, in reverse, all the body language signs and signals you learned in chapter 2, and all the flirting body language you display will be deflected back to you. He'll cross his arms, pull away, minimize eye contact, face away from you, point his body away from you, and cross his legs tightly. In short, his signals are crossed. He has shut down.

It's easy to jump to the conclusion that it was something you did or something about you. But chances are, if he seemed interested at first, it's probably not you and likely beyond your control. Something triggered his reaction along the way, and it's very likely that you will never know exactly what it was. Perhaps his ex walked into the room, or he heard a song, a word, or a phrase that reminded him of something upsetting. Maybe some aspect of your personality reminds him of someone he misses in a sad way, or someone he dislikes. Does he seem embarrassed? He's attracted to someone else. Cautious? He might think that you're with someone else, maybe a friend you arrived with.

Especially if his mood change is abrupt, don't take it personally. You may have triggered it, but it definitely wasn't you who caused his feelings to change. If you want, you can attempt to remedy the situation— ask if he's feeling okay. But if he is deeply upset he won't want to talk, and you need to let it go and feel good that you tried to be nice.

But then again, maybe the guy you sussed out to flirt with is a jerk. It's possible that you picked a guy with ego issues, and he's playing mind games with you (or anyone else who comes along). Really insecure people have big, sensitive, overblown egos, and one of the ways they puff themselves up to feel important and powerful is to make other people feel bad. Really.

So maybe you picked a bad apple. Toss him back and pick a sweeter one.

Another possibility is that he simply changed his mind. It's easy to think someone looks cute and you get close, only to realize that you shouldn't be cruising when your sweetie is out of town, or find that your flirtee likes something you secretly hate, or wears silver and you only like gold jewelry—you get my drift. Pulling out is not the most mature reaction to a flirting situation, but people do it all the time, and sometimes it's going to happen to you. There's nothing you can do about it except look for the next potential playmate.

On the other hand, it could be you. Nothing wrong with you personally, but perhaps your radar was off for a minute or two and you thought his "come hither" look was a sure thing when he was actually just staring off into space and you happened to be dead center in his sights. Make sure you review the clues and cues in this book carefully before you flirt, and look for more than a few signals at a time to be sure his light has turned green for your approach. (See chapter 4.) There is the possibility that something about you caused him to change his mind, and that's when you check yourself in the mirror, or check in with a friend to see how you look, sound, and act. If anything, it's nice to hear that you look hot and that the cold fish you were trying to warm up was really just a flounder.

DON'T DO IT:

▸ Depend on other people to have a good time.

▸ Flirt while wasted, really drunk, stoned, trashed, depressed, stressed out, or mad.

▸ Look bored.

▸ Negatively tease your flirt target.

▸ Freeze up, verbally or physically.

▸ Point at him when gesturing.

▸ Talk about how hot or sexy another guy is.

▸ Interrupt him a lot.

▸ Talk about exes.

Flirt Fails and Fixes

———

Flirting missteps are sometimes unavoidable. When you've stepped in it, there's not much you can do except play it cool. Some flirt accidents can be cleaned up, and others need to be abandoned by the side of the road. Refer to the following problems and solutions to help you navigate flirting's inevitable messy mishaps.

PROBLEM: You made a joke and he's not laughing.

SOLUTION: Maybe he didn't hear you, or maybe he's okay with pretending he didn't. Don't repeat what might have been, for whatever reason, inappropriate; instead, roll with it and change the topic. Keep the conversation moving by asking him something on a different subject altogether. His reaction to your questions will let you know how stinky your accident was, and if conversation keeps flowing (and recovery seems slow but possible), you'll be okay. If your questions are met with silence, minimal eye contact, or worse (he insults you or becomes mean), let this guy go.

PROBLEM: His attention is wandering.

SOLUTION: Well, you could always expose a breast. Ask him a question that requires a thoughtful reply, such as:

"What is your relationship with the host?"

"How do you like to spend your free time?"

"Are you a virgin?"

PROBLEM: Something unladylike came out of your [nose / other orifice].

SOLUTION: Accuse someone else, loudly and immediately.

PROBLEM: You realize you're oversharing, talking too fast, or blathering on like a ninny.

SOLUTION: Breathe. Laugh. Smile. Ask if you're using up all the oxygen, and ask him a question, Motormouth.

PROBLEM: You trip, drop your cell phone in the dip, or step on the host's cat / Pekingese / infant.

SOLUTION: Take a deep bow and dance around like

a loon. Seriously—smile, and look as sexy as possible cleaning up your mess.

PROBLEM: Nature is calling and if you do not answer her immediately, all bets are off.

SOLUTION: Always plan ahead by having a card with your contact info on it—not your personal, private email and cell number, but an email address that you create just for meeting strangers, with no actual personal information on the account. Hand him a card, say something mysterious about your minions or a breakthrough at your secret laboratory, and dash off, leaving him in a cloud of intrigue. *Who was that enigmatic, alluring, obviously important, and slightly sweaty femme fatale?*

9

TEASES, TRAPS, AND FLIRTING WITH SUCCESS

Being a flirt is more than just learning a few bad-girl tricks to have a hot time at a party. It's for good girls, bad girls, and every girl who wants to glow a bit brighter than the rest—and every girl who wants to be able to make that connection when she finds the guy who's worth it. It's a power strut, it's a night out with your posse, it's how you know the morning after that you're celebrating your life. It's a fun game well worth playing, whether you flirt for fun or you flirt with intent.

But you're not the only one who might be out flirting with a goal in mind. There are benefits to knowing what techniques other people are using—in addition to how to get your goal when you find the guy. To be a flirting supervixen or keep your sweetheart status, it pays to know that there is a large, worldwide community of male "pickup artists" out there who have a lot of ideas about how to snag a girl. One of their mantras is "always closing": from Minute One they are trying to "close the deal" to get you into bed. And letting them do all the work is fine if that's what you want. But when it's your turn to "close the deal," read this chapter for ways to make him yours and keep all your saucy sweetness from going to waste.

The "Secret Society" of Pickup Artists

For as long as boys have watched James Bond movies and wanted to pull Bond moves on girls to get us in the sack, there have been piles of literature and oodles of online message boards about how to fool girls with pickup tricks. Most famously, author Neil Strauss wrote a book titled *The Game* where he went undercover (sort of) and infiltrated the so-called secret society of pickup artists (or PUAs for short). In the book he revealed many of their tricks and strategies, and also how kind of sad they are, but it's great reading and it was consumed by women who didn't want to end up manipulated into bed by a non-Bond.

Like villains conjured up by Austin Powers, PUAs have code words, techniques that are a lot like gaming structures, and a slew of dirty "secret weapon" methods, personas, and nicknames. (The fluffy white cat is optional.) They have no fembots, and that's the problem.

The Game, and How Not to Get Played

So what kinds of tricks do these guys use? Hall of scary mirrors? Surprise alligator pit of doom? Doomsday device? No, they've got lots of tricks, but believe me: if they could use a time machine, a voodoo doll, or an invisibility potion, they would. These poor wannabe Love Gurus have worked on refining every trick they can think of, and some of their tricks are pretty effective—and pretty low. The pickup artist spends more time in front of the mirror before going out than you do, and he's usually got a posse of henchmen to back his plays. But don't forget what you read in chapter 1: the rules of the game are clear—girls control the game, even when boys think they're in charge. Here's a handy guide to spotting the elements of their strategy, in the order they play it. This is the template for pickup artist techniques:

1. **PICK A TARGET.** (That's you!)

2. **APPROACH AND OPEN.** (Pickup lines.)

3. **SHOW VALUE.** (Gets your attention with a cheap trick.)

4. **DISARM OBSTACLES.** (He befriends any person with you who seems "in charge.")

5. **ISOLATE.** (Separates you from your friends.)

6. **MAKE EMOTIONAL CONNECTION.** (Gets you to talk about emotions, agrees with you.)

7. **RELOCATE.** (Gets you alone to get your panties off.)

Here are some wannabe pickup artist personas, and real techniques they'll try out on you:

BLONDE. JAMES BLONDE.

SECRET WEAPON: Opening lines you don't expect. Negs (negative compliments), cold reading (pretending he knows more about you than you do by observing details about you), made-up lines ("Did you see the fight outside?"). Demonstrations of higher value.

HIS STYLE: For decades Mr. Blonde has disarmed ladies around the globe by telling them their teeth are crooked before saying anything nice about them, or saying he can "tell" something about you (you're smart, interesting, etc.) by a detail of your appearance (your jewelry). Blonde's goal is to get you talking to him by baiting the conversation with things you don't understand, or by making you feel less confident.

THE LOVE GURU

SECRET WEAPON: Emotional connection. Getting you to open up after devaluing you, and agreeing with your feelings.

HIS STYLE: It's all in the love beads, baby! The Love Guru likes to tell you that you don't seem happy, and then ask you what makes you really happy. No, really happy. As if you'd tell any old Love Guru what makes you really happy deep down inside. But any feelings you share with LG he'll agree with, to establish a connection with you that cancels out the competition.

DAVID BLAINE, AKA DAVID LAME

SECRET WEAPON: Mind control. Dark arts, including hypnosis techniques, power of suggestion through words.

HIS STYLE: Mr. Lame thinks he's studied magic and hypnosis so he can get any girl into bed, and he probably really has spent many lonely nights reading about how to use the power of suggestion to make you think that getting it on with him was all your idea in the first place. He's been studying something called Neuro-Linguistic Programming, a technique in psychology also seen in stage magic routines. He persuades you that he's The Man because he acts like you both *already know* he's the man.

THE D-LISTER

SECRET WEAPON: Devaluing himself. Pretending he thinks he's not as cool or sexy as others so you will reassure him that he is and consider him harmless. Wearing a "flair," a feminine or even outrageous accessory that makes him seem more interesting or accessible than male-model types, who he knows intimidate you.

HIS STYLE: This guy is such a D-lister he'd show up to attend the opening of a bag of chips, and he wants you to know it! His idea is that girls value things they have to work for, and that by being self-deprecating (like jokingly agreeing with your teasing), he'll disarm you. By seeming to be convinced of his shortcomings, he'll make you work to convince him of his worth— convincing yourself in the process. His flair (also called "peacocking")—like Brad Pitt wearing rose-colored shades and a fur coat in *Fight Club*—adds to the confidence game.

Their Tricks, Remixed for Flirt Fatales

If the pickup artist's tricks sound complicated, that's because they are! Girls who get what they want, whether we're feeling naughty or nice, wicked or sweet, know that it doesn't take any more than a warm smile, a little eye contact, and a sexy pair of shoes. Stick a fork in him, Vixen—he's done.

That doesn't mean you can't have a little fun with the pickup artist techniques, as restyled for girls. Are there female PUAs? Yes, there are, and they form posses to go out and cruise in major cities all over the world. So, why not try out the boys' techniques on—the boys? It takes some translation, but you won't get lost in it. Just remember that you already have the upper hand (thanks, researchers); you only need to decide when your fun and games goes from fun to intentional, and how far you want to go with any of the boys' own "dirty tricks" and negative techniques that they like to use on us girls. Turning the tables is not only a lot of fun—it works. You decide how bad you want to be.

There's no reason you can't form your own posse and make a night of it. Compare opening lines, compare men, egg each other on to try out a Pussycat Walk across the pub, or see if your BFF has the guts to try out her smile sorcery on the delicious guy at the other side of the party. Do it! Make a party plan.

THE GIRLS' PUA SAFARI PARTY

Every girl loves a safari: especially when the wild animals are guys and you're all on the hunt.

WHAT YOU NEED: This book, your hot friends, and a club where the boys are poppin'.

PREP: Invite 3–4 of your fun-loving girlfriends over and get your "game faces" on. Play rallying music, sip beverages, and discuss world domination plans.

WHAT TO DO: Practice your Pussycat Walk for each other before you go out. Make an entrance, and then stake out your central spot. Go over the Flirt Mode checklist together. Get your drinks and discuss targets: you're on a safari—what's the wildlife like? Each one of you has to make one trip to approach and try an opener on the guy of her choosing, and make an exit. She must then return to the group with a status report, and friends take turns giving suggestions on how it went and what to do next. (Bag and tag, or catch and release?) Repeat until the male drool quotient is out of control.

Ask yourself: what do you want? A one-night stand? To look hot in front of your friends, strangers, that guy with the phone taking pictures? Or do you want a date? The world is your oyster now that you've got the flirting checklists to die for, and with your mad skills the men will be lining up for you like pearls to make a necklace out of. The toughest thing you have left to do is choose which one you want, and decide what to do next.

In chapter 8, Miss Titanic: Avoid a Flirting Disaster, we saw the many ways you can hit the Eject button and say "Get me outta here" without actually having to pretend that you left your eight children in the car with all the windows rolled up on a summer day. Basically, you can pick and choose your exits and your closes. This depends on what you want, how the vibe feels, how many of your girlfriends are watching and holding up scorecards, and whether you want to take him home now or see him later.

Turn Up the Heat: Rules of the Tease

———

This book is all about getting what you want: bad girl, good girl, it's all the same when you can turn heads as you walk into a bar and get fame and love and fortune and parking spots and all the instant gratification you want with the bat of your lashes. You've read the checklists, the rules of engagement, and you even know surefire strategies for VIPing your way to the front of the line leading to the hottest guy in the room.

You're living *La Vida Flirta*. While you celebrate life with free drinks from bees attracted by your honey, you'll want to know how to keep the heat rising and not be pegged as a total tease. But you want to be *just enough* of a tease to make it fun for everyone. A power tease never offers anything she can't or won't deliver. Learn the teasing rule *when* not *if*: the art of teasing depends on *when* you'll give him whatever you're dangling in front of him (a kiss? a date?), not *if* it's going to happen at all.

A good tease takes all the flirtatious signals and signs from this book and puts them on Shuffle >

Repeat for the duration, baby. Once you've got him in your sights, don't let him off the hook! A good tease also teases her target gently about his uniquenesses, and never insults, or teases about touchy subjects like his difficult past as a sow inseminator.

The best teases are never in a hurry; don't rush anything. The more you talk, the more you'll want to slooowly move in a little bit closer. Crank up the heat by speaking a little lower, and leaning in so he can hear you at a crucial point in the conversation.

Close the Deal and Flirt with Success

———

Make him now, or take him later? The choice is yours. You want to provide him with windows of opportunity either to make plans with you now or to get together another night. Things to say when you want to see him again include:

▸ "We're not sure what we're doing later."

▸ "What do you do for fun on the weekends?"

▸ "I should go explain to my friends where I am. Do you want to come meet them?"

▸ "Oh, by the way, I do [x] too. Here's my [email address / Twitter handle]."

▸ "Do you guys know a good place to go after this?"

▸ "I haven't seen a movie in a theater in ages. Are there any good ones playing?"

▸ "Wow, if only there was some way we could stay in touch!"

▸ "Are you this much fun when you're sober?"
(Bonus points if he doesn't drink.)

If life is a cupcake, being a Flirt Fatale is the frosting on top. Your sweet skills are your ticket to ride, your backstage pass, your upgrade to first class on the best flight in the skies. What you've gleaned in this book is more than a bag of tricks; it's the secret that makes your sauce saucier. It's how to get what you want. Use your skills with flair, with respect, and with love for your posse. Now go out and make it happen.

Note to the Reader

———

Find new tips and tricks, phone apps to guide you through in-the-field flirting, video how-tos, and much more to go along with everything in this book at **TheTotalFlirt.com**. Special for *Total Flirt* readers: enter the first and last words of chapter 3 as your passcode to receive a downloadable bonus chapter of more pickup lines, exit strategies, and suggestions for how to turn flirting into dating.

Violet **Blue** (tinynibbles.com, techyum.com @ violetblue) is a Forbes Web Celeb and one of Wired's Faces of Innovation—in addition to being a blogger, a high-profile tech personality, and an infamous podcaster. Violet has written many award-winning, best-selling books; an excerpt from her book *The Smart Girl's Guide to Porn* is featured on Oprah Winfrey's website. She is regarded as the fore-most expert in the field of sex and technology. Violet is a sex-positive pundit in mainstream media (CNN, *The Oprah Winfrey Show*, *The Tyra Banks Show*) and is regularly interviewed, quoted, and featured prominently by major media outlets. A published feature writer and columnist since 1998, she writes for media outlets such as *Mac Life* magazine, *O: The Oprah Magazine*, and the UN-sponsored international health organization RH Reality Check. She was the notorious sex columnist for the *San Francisco Chronicle*, writing the weekly column "Open Source Sex." She headlines at conferences ranging from ETech, LeWeb, and SXSW: Interactive to Google Tech Talks at Google, Inc. The *London Times* named Blue "one of the 40 bloggers who really count."

TO OUR READERS

Viva Editions publishes books that inform, enlighten, and entertain. We do our best to bring you, the reader, quality books that celebrate life, inspire the mind, revive the spirit, and enhance lives all around. Our authors are practical visionaries: people who offer deep wisdom in a hopeful and helpful manner. Viva was launched with an attitude of growth and we want to spread our joy and offer our support and advice where we can to help you live the Viva way: vivaciously!

We're grateful for all our readers and want to keep bringing you books for inspired living. We invite you to write to us with your comments and suggestions, and what you'd like to see more of. You can also sign up for our online newsletter to learn about new titles, author events, and special offers.

Viva Editions
2246 Sixth St.
Berkeley, CA 94710
www.vivaeditions.com
(800) 780-2279
Follow us on Twitter @vivaeditions
Friend/fan us on Facebook